Religion and
Personal Autonomy

Studies in Comparative Religion
Frederick M. Denny, Editor

Religion and Personal Autonomy

The Third Disestablishment in America

PHILLIP E. HAMMOND

University of South Carolina Press

Published in Columbia, South Carolina, by the
University of South Carolina Press

Manufactured in the United States of America

Library of Congress Cataloging-in-Publication Data

Hammond, Phillip E.
    Religion and personal autonomy : the third disestablishment in
America / Phillip E. Hammond.
        p.   cm.
    Includes bibliographical references and index.
    ISBN 0-87249-820-4
    1. United States—Religion—1960- 2. Sociology, Christian—United
States—History—20th century.   I. Title.
BR526.H25   1992
261.8'34'0973—dc20   91-46356

To the Ocean Meadows Three

Contents

Series Editor's Preface

The comparative study of religion, particularly its more humanistic and phenomenological varieties, has not been known for quantitative interests. But since the inception of this series, we have attempted to cross traditional boundaries by publishing a wide variety of comparative scholarship. Phillip E. Hammond's *Religion and Personal Autonomy: The Third Disestablishment in America* is very much a comparative and historical as well as quantitative sociological inquiry into beliefs, attitudes, and values of Americans.

Hammond has discovered that institutional forms of religion—church and synagogue—have, since the 1960s, come to be viewed increasingly by Americans as optional, "individual-expressive" agencies rather than as inherited and commanding "collective-expressive" agencies. The "first disestablishment" of American religion, embodied in the First Amendment to the Constitution of the United States, did not keep organized religion from wielding enormous influence in the public sector of American life. But the source of that influence, a pervasive Protestant establishment, lost its position of supremacy in a "second disestablishment" that came about between the two world wars. From the 1930s to the 1960s institutional religion—Catholic, Jewish, Protestant—continued to influence political and governmental affairs in America, but since the 1960s personal autonomy has grown to the point where the older "collective-expressive" entities, particularly the "mainline" denominations, have experienced a steep decline both in membership and influence.

Hammond has found that, although religion is still important among Americans, because of the increase in personal autonomy it most often finds expression in private, individual ways, whether within the old institutional forms or in newer movements—some radically countercultural, others more traditional but non-indigenous—that have found many adherents. The consequences of this "third disestablishment," as Hammond calls it, have already proved fateful for organized religion's influence in the public sectors of American life as well as for its relationship to identity and individual values within an increasingly multicultural ethos.

Although Hammond's study relates to the present day, it brings to mind concerns of religion and the public order that have resonated in America since colonial times. Jonathan Edwards's subtle and exhaustive investigation of the "holy affections" had as its aim to distinguish what is genuine from what is spurious in religious experience. He concluded that genuine spirituality always finds expression in an obedient and disciplined Christian commitment that, as Muslims so often say of their religion, is a "complete way of life."

The conviction that religion and freedom were both essential to the common life was a hallmark of both colonial and republican American life from John Winthrop through Edwards to Jefferson and well beyond, and it played a central role in defining the American character. Writing a century after Edwards and the "surprising conversions" Edwards's parish experienced in Northampton, the French observer Alexis de Tocqueville marveled at the strong religious piety of Americans which could thrive in a free society where the separation of church and state was absolute. Although the varieties of doctrine, theological opinion, liturgy, communal identity, and institutional governance in the United States were myriad, Tocqueville perceived that most Americans shared a common moral outlook, because their "ethos" and their "world-view"—to apply Clifford Geertz's useful distinction—were both united in a Christian "cultural system." Hammond's findings, however, if they are sustained, will make it difficult any longer to agree with the second part of the following typically confident observation made by Tocqueville in his *De la démocratie en Amérique:* "One is not able therefore to say that in the United States religion influences the laws or the detail of political opinions; *but it does direct mores, and in regulating the family it strives to regulate the state*" (translation and emphasis mine).

Whether Hammond's more than 2,600 interviews across a wide spectrum of denominational affiliations and ethnic and racial identities in California, Massachusetts, North Carolina, and Ohio will be found to have provided sufficient data to sustain his conclusions about a third disestablishment of American religion only time and further research will tell. But a measure of the significance of this study is that before its publication a symposium discussing Hammond's findings was published in the *Journal for the Scientific Study of Religion* (vol. 30, no. 4, December 1991, pp. 515–547).

Frederick Mathewson Denny

Preface

Social scientific monographs—as distinct from textbooks—
dealing with the entire American religious scene have been rare
in this century. For some decades, it seems, both the pluralism
and the dynamism of American religion meant that no single
portrait could capture the whole, and few were attempted.
H. Richard Niebuhr's *Social Sources of Denominationalism* (1929) is
an exception, though his focus was more on Protestantism than
Catholicism or Judaism. Will Herberg's *Protestant, Catholic, Jew*
(1955) is another exception. Both of these books gave us "bench
marks"—standards by which assessments could be made and
change over time judged. It is perhaps significant that the first
book, reflecting primarily on a splintered Christianity in America, was written at a time when all hope had vanished that
America would ever become a "Christian nation," and that the
second book, identifying the religion-in-general then approved
by most Americans, was written just before such religious ho-
mogeneity was severely challenged.

Given the scarcity of such large portraits, therefore, it is remarkable that in a single year two new analyses were offered to
students of American religion. The first was W. Clark Roof and
William McKinney's *American Mainline Religion* (1987), the second Robert Wuthnow's *Restructuring of American Religion* (1988).
Both are broad in scope and empirical at base. One is a system-
atic analysis of massive amounts of survey data, the other a
great synthesis of many kinds of information. Both tell us much
about the current religious scene in America, and they do so
with the use of markedly different, yet noncontradictory,
metaphors.

For Roof and McKinney the metaphor is "the collapse of the
middle," the change that overtook American religion during
and since the 1960s. The mainline consequently became "fragmented." For Wuthnow the effect is similar, but the metaphor

xiii

suggests a somewhat different dynamic—a "great divide" leading to the "religious realignment" of Liberals and Conservatives. The first image has the middle ground crumbling, leaving
left and right fringes and a lot of religious individualism; the
second image has the left and right mobilizing and disengaging
from many arenas once occupied by both.

These two books are persuasive in their arguments and in
their documentation. The present work should not be seen as a
challenge to them, therefore, but as simply another portrait—
one also using a markedly different, yet noncontradictory metaphor to help understand the massive religious shift that has
occurred since the 1960s. My metaphor is "disestablishment," a
notion that gets full treatment ahead. Suffice for now to say that
by disestablishment I am referring to a qualitative change in the
relationship between church and culture. It is my contention
that, despite the voluntary character of churchgoing since colonial days, and despite the legal disestablishment of any church
in any state since 1833, involvement in church life could be said to
have remained normative—and thus "established"—for most
Americans until the 1960s. For a variety of reasons, ever since
the nation's founding, a higher and higher proportion of Americans have affiliated with a church or synagogue—right through
the 1950s. This makes the shift following the 1960s seem more
abrupt than it would have seemed had it occurred in, say, the
Depression years or the 1940s war years. The shift, moreover,
was expressed not just in the peaking—and, in some cases, the
decline—of parish involvement but, what is more important
culturally, the symbolic role of that involvement changed.

This change over is my main focus, but the degree of pre–
1960s "establishment" to be "disestablished" differed by denomination and by region. Hence, the abruptness of the shift
can be highlighted by showing where it has been felt least as
well as where it has been felt most.

The data on which my argument rests come from telephone
surveys with 2,620 adults, randomly selected in the states of
Massachusetts, North Carolina, Ohio, and California. (The interview schedule is reproduced as Appendix B. Readers not fa-
miliar with reports of quantitative social research may also find

helpful Appendix C: The Research Process.) I was joined by W. Clark Roof and John Shelton Reed in preparing the questionnaire, though I am solely responsible for the present analysis, they being involved in other analyses of this survey. The Lilly Endowment and its then vice-president Robert Wood Lynn supported my research. Since Lynn's retirement I have enjoyed also the support of his successor, Craig Dykstra. The Interdisciplinary Humanities Center on the UCSB campus administered the grant, and my thanks go to its director, Paul Hernadi, and its administrative assistant, Randi Glick.

Several graduate students in religious studies and sociology also gave me assistance, including Michael Dilucci, Phillip Lucas, Richard Merkel, and Brian Wilson. Mark Shibley was my patient and efficient research assistant for the several years from the inception of the research to its completion. He will be relieved to get on with his own research, a reward richly deserved.

Sara Duke also deserves reward for her cheerful preparation of the many drafts of this manuscript.

One category in the research budget of the grant from the Lilly Endowment permitted a group of us interested in region and religion to assemble for five different weekends over three years' time, alternatively in Santa Barbara and Berkeley. That group consisted of Catherine Albanese, Eldon Ernst, Ardith Hayes, J. Gordon Melton, Robert Michaelsen, W. Clark Roof, Barbara Brown Zikmund, and myself. As might be surmised, I benefited greatly from these seminar-workshops.

As for the Ocean Meadows Three—Bob Palmer, John Perea, Barbara Sutcliffe—they may find the dedication of a book an odd way to be thanked, but they will know what for.

Religion and
Personal Autonomy

Chapter One

The Process of
Disestablishment

During a summer weekend every year in Santa Barbara, a Greek Festival is held in one of the city parks.[1] The booths selling souvlaki and dolmas are operated by—and for the benefit of—the Greek Orthodox parish in town. And this sponsorship is prominently displayed by a sign on each booth. In 1986 something interesting could be noted about those signs. Carefully and beautifully printed, they announced the sponsor as "The Greek Church of Santa Barbara." Then inscribed in longhand, between the words "Greek" and "Church," someone had added "Orthodox." Whoever first prepared the signs, in other words, had failed to mention the part of the label that, in substance, is of greatest importance: What church is sponsoring this booth? The Greek *Orthodox* Church!

Of course nobody was misled or in doubt. Perhaps only perverse sociologists of religion would even notice. But something interesting was implied by the original omission: The signmaker, while acknowledging by choice of words that there could be Greek sponsorship which is *not* the church, was also implying that churchgoing Greeks in Santa Barbara go to *one church only.*

Such is one view of the church—that it is more or less dictated by one's primary group allegiances. And not just dictated by, but expressive of, those allegiances. Indeed, in the original formulation by Ernst Troeltsch (1911) the "church," as distinct from the "sect," is something one is born into rather than voluntarily

---

1. This chapter is a revised version of a presidential address to the Society for the Scientific Study of Religion (Hammond, 1988). In that address I advanced a thesis regarding the changing role of the church in America since the 1960s. At the time I had hope that the Lilly Endowment would fund the research necessary to test the thesis. It did, and this book is the result. A comparison of the address with this chapter will reveal where modifications in the thesis have occurred.

1

joining. In America, no doubt, this view of the church was strongest in the nineteenth century, when ethnicity, immigrant status, and various aspects of socioeconomic status all over-lapped. By now the church decreasingly plays this "collective-expressive" role, even if exceptions may remain, as the Santa Barbara Greek Festival would suggest. After all, fewer and fewer of us are embedded in primary groups, and—what may be more important—the few primary group ties we do have are not overlapping. Instead, as the classic sociological formulation has it, we are chiefly involved in a series of seg-mented relationships.

For many therefore—especially those not embedded in pri-mary groups—the church is simply one of these segmented re-lationships. Far from expressing collective ties, the church is one of the ways by which individuals (often joined by other members of their nuclear families) may try to cope with this seg-mented life. Very much a voluntary association for such people, the religious organization represents for them not an inherited relationship but a relationship that can be entered and left with little or no impact on their other relationships. Church for them is not simultaneously a gathering of kin, neighbors, fellow workers, and leisure-time friends but rather a separate activity, expressing another meaning. For such people it is not a neces-sary moral compass, an anchorage in a world of conflicting ex-pectations, but rather a safe harbor, one place to sort out life's dilemmas. If such people do get involved in a church, they are therefore more likely to do so for their *own* reasons, even if they have friendly relations there. Their view of the church might therefore be called "individual-expressive." Put another way, whereas others may regard the church as a natural extension of their social worlds, these people regard it as an avenue to some privately chosen goal—for example, to commune with God, ed-ucate their children religiously, enjoy music, or get therapy.

Of course, just as persons with an individual-expressive view of the church may have friends in the church, so may pri-vate goals be held by those for whom the church is collective-expressive. But whereas the former will likely withdraw their participation if their goals are not met, the latter are likely to maintain their church involvement irrespective of their personal agendas. For them, to put it simply, the church is not an object that they, as individuals, may freely accept or reject.

Of course, this characterization is exaggerated. No population can be divided neatly into two churchgoing groups: one that "must" go and another that "chooses" to go. How much pressure one feels—and the nature of the obligation felt as a result—will differ from one person to another. At the same time, so will the freedom to choose—and the way *it* is felt—differ from person to person. Thus, over and beyond the view of the church carried by persons is the set of circumstances peculiar to each as they live their lives, sensitive now to some people, beholden to others, oblivious to yet others.

Throughout, however, the church as a social institution maintains a cultural status quite independent of any individual's peculiar circumstances. In Santa Barbara the Greek Orthodox Church exists and has a more-or-less agreed-upon meaning, at least for Greek-Americans in the region, and no single dissenting view is likely to alter that meaning. That is to say, if full participation in the Santa Barbara Greek-American community stipulated involvement in the Greek Orthodox Church, then noninvolvement—while legally permissible, of course—would be deviant. Persons choosing to be uninvolved would factor into their sense of self such noninvolvement, and, perhaps as important, so would others. The collectivity would still be expressed by the church, but in this case the uninvolved would lie to some extent "outside" this collectivity.

Likewise in the individual-expressive case. Even though a church recognizes that most of its members are strangers to each other, other members may regard that church as the social center of their lives. Here, for example, is an announcement from the bulletin of a church that, though it has a small nucleus of longtime members well known to each other, fits the model of an individual-expressive church:

> The Evangelism Committee wants to provide everyone with an easy way to make contact with both visitors and familiar faces. Just take an extra second or two on your way to coffee hour following the service to write your name on a tag, and then

say hello to someone whose name you'd just been waiting to
know. One Sunday per month will be designated CONTACT
SUNDAY. On that day, everyone in the church is to discover
at least one new fact about someone else at coffee hour. It could
be her/his name, occupation, the number of years a member of
St. Paul's . . . whatever.

Imagine two people discovering that both have been members
for years, yet they have not met, not learned each other's name,
nor otherwise shared a "community" in all that time. Surely
this church for them, if it is important, is important in the
individual-expressive sense.

Religion and Identity

The distinction we are making—between the church as more
collective-expressive or more individual-expressive—has a parallel in what role the church may play in how people think of
themselves. The "identities" of both types may be informed by
religion, but they will be differently informed, as the two concepts of identity used in the social sciences would suggest (Mol
1978). One way of looking at identity suggest the immutable—
or at least the slowly changing—core of personality that shows
up in all of a person's encounters, irrespective of differing role
partners. The second way suggests the transient and change-
able self as persons move from one social encounter to another,
offering a somewhat different identity, as it were, in each place.
The first notion of identity suggests that it is involuntarily held;
the second, that it can be put on and off. The first is nourished
in primary groups, probably early in life; the second exists precisely because much of life is lived in arenas outside of primary
groups.

About these two notions of identity, the following observations might be made: 1) Both notions can be appropriate and
therefore useful. 2) Some institutional spheres—most notably
the family—are inevitably important in the first sense, while
other institutional spheres—most notably the workplace—are
inevitably important in the second sense, though they may be
important in the first sense as well. 3) Some institutional
spheres—and here is where we are locating contemporary
churches—may, in modern societies, be shifting from being im-

portant primarily in the first sense to being important primarily in the second sense. If in fact such a shift is occurring, the consequences for the church may be considerable. That issue is the subject of this book. While the shift we have in mind has been occurring for a long time, it is the thesis here that the social revolution of the 1960s and '70s speeded up this shift considerably—so much so that it warrants the designation "third disestablishment." We shall turn to that thesis presently, but first some more comments about religion and identity.

We have already noted about the first kind of identity that it is involuntary—that it is thrust upon its possessor by so many others, in so many circumstances, for such a long time, that even if one wanted to escape it, one could not. The phenomenon of "passing" (e.g., of a black as white, a Jew as Gentile)—now no longer much noted—illustrated by its poignancy this essentially involuntary character; one chose to discard an identity of the first sort at great social risk, of course, but also at great psychic cost because this was no facade being peeled away but a pulling out of roots.

Now, it was Durkheim's great insight that religion is born out of the social circumstances providing those involuntary roots (Durkheim 1961). People are led, he said, to represent their sense of unity in the groups of which they are members—to express that unity in ceremony and symbol, in belief and ritual. In the case of the central Australian aborigines he studied, there was no choice in the matter.

Because modern society so little resembles the Australian outback, and because the religions Durkheim described so little resemble religions of our day, we may too easily dismiss this Durkheimian insight as no longer applicable. But that would be a mistake. What can be granted is that, in societies of the sort about which Durkheim wrote, religion was coextensive with social life, and that situation no longer exists anywhere in the modern world. But we must recognize that even in modern society, the church may still be an expression of primary group ties, especially if those ties are to overlapping groups. That is the possible significance of the Greek Festival in Santa Barbara—the maintenance of the first kind of religion-and-identity relationship.

At the same time, however, we must also recognize that for others the church is a secondary association—a voluntary activity that may be switched on and off. Under these circumstances the church may be very important to some people, and thus a source of identity for them; but the identity provided will be an identity of the second sort.

This theoretical viewpoint regarding religion and identity has been well stated by Thomas Luckmann. At one extreme, he says—the extreme at which Durkheim was theorizing—there is congruence among "church, the sacred cosmos, and the hierarchy of meaning in the world view" (1967, 79). As a result, public institutions "significantly contribute to the formation of individual consciousness and personality" (1967, 97). Once there occurs the "institutional specialization of religion," however, the relationship of the individual to the sacred cosmos and social order is transformed, and two hypothetical possibilities are the result (1967, 80):

> In view of this situation [the "institutional specialization of religion"] it is useful to regard church religiosity in two different perspectives. First, we may view church religiosity as a survival of a traditional social form of religion [i.e., the collective-expressive view]. . . . Second, we may view church religiosity as one of many manifestations of an emerging, institutionally nonspecialized social form of religion, the difference being that it still occupies a special place . . . because of its historical connections to the traditional . . . model [i.e., the individual-expressive view]. (1967, 100–101)

Indeed, in the second of these situations the individual is alone "in choosing goods and services, friends, marriage partners, neighbors, hobbies, and . . . even 'ultimate' meanings. . . . In a manner of speaking, he is free to construct his own personal identity" (1967, 98).[2]

To a remarkable degree this perspective on the changing cultural role of churches in America has a parallel in the area of

---

2. A related theoretical perspective on the role of churches in people's lives is often called the "meaning-vs.-belonging" perspective, summarized neatly in McGuire (1987, 23–36).

ethnicity. For some ethnic groups the badge of membership is so clearly marked by such visible characteristics of skin color, hair style, or shape of eyes that persons possessing the badge will be identified—and identify themselves—as belonging to one or another ethnic group. For them ethnicity is likely to provide a primary identity, and they will see themselves as "representatives" of an ethnic collectivity. For others the visible marks are less pronounced, being perhaps a "foreign" name, speech with an accent, or residence in an ethnic neighborhood. In these cases the chances that ethnicity will provide a primary identity are diminished, partly because some social encounters do not require name, speech, or knowledge of residence. Whether, in these cases, persons are expressing membership in an ethnic community or instead are expressing their individual selves is thus importantly dictated by the social context.

But there are yet others for whom ethnicity is entirely voluntary. Whether ethnic identity even enters the exchange will depend upon the wishes of the individuals involved. Under these circumstances ethnic identity automatically becomes individual-expressive, and chances are great that such identity will be secondary rather than primary. As Mary C. Waters, discussing the case of middle-class, white ethnics, puts it:

> Ethnicity is increasingly a personal choice of whether to be ethnic at all, and, for an increasing majority of people, of which ethnicity to be. An ethnic identity is something that does not affect much in everyday life. It does not, for the most part, limit choice of marriage partner. . . . It does not determine where you will live, who your friends will be, what job you will have, or whether you will be subject to discrimination. It matters only in voluntary ways. (1990, 147)

The situation with respect to the cultural role of churches—whether collective-expressive or individual-expressive, whether providing primary identity or secondary identity—is similar. And also like ethnicity, a discernible shift has taken place.

The thesis here is that the social revolution of the 1960s and 1970s accelerated the shifting balance of these two views of the church, doing so by greatly escalating a phenomenon we will call "personal autonomy." Personal autonomy thus has not only led to a decline in parish involvement—by increased individual-over collective-expressiveness and increased secondary over primary identity—but it has also led to an alteration in the meaning of that involvement. The result we are calling the "third disestablishment."

The Process of Disestablishment

It is true that, in the legal sense, the United States has never had a national established church. Nonetheless, churches, especially Protestant churches, have historically enjoyed a kind of "establishment" status in American culture. Their leaders have been community leaders, for example, and, in the nineteenth century especially, they were prominent in what Donald Mathews called "an organizing process"—the establishment of schools, hospitals, orphanages, colleges, magazines, etc. (1969, 23–24). It might be said, therefore, that churches once played a significant role in the first kind of identity formation of many people, even if that role was being overtaken by the second kind of identity formation. What might be further noted, and as the above discussion on identity formation would suggest, to the degree the individual-expressive view of churches was replacing the collective-expressive view, the effect was a decline in their "establishment" status, that is, a reduction in the public linkage of religion with social collectivities. The change, in brief, was a step toward "disestablishment." The *legal* situation had not changed, of course, since in the eyes of the law no churches were ever established nationally (in 1833 Massachusetts became the final state to dismantle its tax-supported religious activity). But, as we will now review, the disestablishment process has been occurring right along, though churches and the American people have experienced it not smoothly but in jolts—at times when the disestablishment shift has been accelerated.

The first jolt, we may surmise, took place with the adoption of the Bill of Rights. Actually the jolt must have preceded the Constitution because historians agree that no serious effort was made by any denomination at the time of the nation's founding to gain favored status by law. As Sidney Mead writes:

When the American Revolution was completed, let us say with John Adams by around 1815, not only had the Established Church of England been rejected, but, more important, the very idea of "Establishment" had been discarded in principle by the new Constitution. (1977, 76)

Roger Finke states the case somewhat differently:

With the new rules of law, upstart sects and new religions were not only given a right to exist (toleration), they were given "equal" rights; and the once privileged religious establishments lost the legislative and financial support of the state. By denying the establishment of any religion, and granting the free exercise of religion to all, they could no longer support regulation that denied privileges to or imposed sanctions on specific religious organizations—or their members. The state was denied the privilege, and freed of the obligation, of regulating religion. (1990, 609)

What followed in the nineteenth century was nevertheless, for all intents and purposes, a continued Protestant "establishment"—a kind of "American Christendom," as Eldon Ernst labels it.

Protestants conceived of an American Christian democracy infused by their church traditions. . . . Protestant-dominated politics, from fugitive slave laws to know-nothing nativist elections to prohibition legislation, was geared to protect white Anglo-Saxon Protestant civilization. The arts, economics, politics, even war, bore the Protestant imprint. (1987, 151)

Of course, this hegemonic position of Protestantism was challenged, not least by the massive immigration of Roman Catholics, whose leaders had their own image of an "American Christendom."

But no sooner had Catholics come of age in America than they, along with Protestants, would find themselves plunged into a whole new quest for their Christian identity in a post-Christendom environment. . . . Historically, the demise of Protestant America can be traced most precisely to the period of World War I and the changing temper of life in the 1920s. (Ernst 1987, 154, 156)

The consequence thus was a second jolt, appropriately called by Robert Handy "the second disestablishment":

The hopes for a Christian America as envisioned by nineteenth-century evangelicals were fast fading in the face of the realities of postwar America; the enthusiasm and morale needed to sustain the crusade were undermined. . . . The prestige of Protestantism was further lessened by the bitter controversy between fundamentalists and modernists (1984, 169, 175–76).

Following the religious downturn of the 1920s, the economic depression of the 1930s, and the disruption of a second World War, churches bounced back, and among those bouncing back were Protestant churches, of course. But the second step toward disestablishment was not reversed. Instead, even with record-setting memberships, attendance, and church construction— taken by some to mean a "revival," the authenticity of which was much debated—churches found themselves popular but less powerful. More precisely, they enjoyed greater popularity than ever before, but they were reduced in their role as carriers of American values to being more custodial than directorial. Needless to say, Protestants felt this loss more keenly because they had once uniquely played that role, but the disestablishment of religious organizations in the sense of a declining public presence was true for all churches. By the 1950s this alteration in the relationship between churches and the sociopolitical culture was becoming clear. As Will Herberg's *Protestant, Catholic, Jew* (1955) helped us see, the vast majority of Americans were committed to a tolerant, bland religion that happened to come in three major flavors. The choice was theirs. The potential for a new blossoming of the individual-expressive church was therefore great.

The Third Disestablishment

The third jolt is what Roof and McKinney call "the collapse of the religious and cultural middle" and thus the loss of religion's "integrative force." They even suggest that this collapse represents a possible "third disestablishment" (1987, 33–39). Religion, they say, may be no less visible in American life, but now it is more likely to divide than to integrate. In other words, religion since the 1960s, to the degree it is important, is more likely to be *individually* important and less likely to be *collectively* important. We concur in this assessment and agree, moreover, that it marks such a change from the previous decades as to warrant the label "third disestablishment." Probably, too, it is in the social revolution of the 1960s and '70s where we find the major cause of this third jolt, this further radical shift in the balance of collective-expressive and individual-expressive views of the church. The mechanism of the social revolution by which this radical shift came about will be called here "personal autonomy," a view of life that gained such strength during this time.

Personal Autonomy

Nobody doubts that some sort of "revolution" took place in the 1960s and 1970s. Debate may exist over how much took place, the forms it took, and what it should be called, but few would deny that radical changes occurred during this period, changes that were adopted by many and resisted by others. (In addition to works already cited in the preface, the following offer important views of the 1960s–'70s revolution: Bibby 1987; Cox 1965; Fitzgerald 1986; McLoughlin 1978; Neuhaus 1984.) We suggest that these changes, taken together, can be understood as a significant increase in "personal autonomy," meaning both an enlarged arena of voluntary choice and an enhanced freedom from structural restraint. Many ways of doing and thinking were changed, and the changes were in the direction of greater individual autonomy.[3]

Two areas of change—quite distinct and unrelated but both having considerable impact on people's view of the church and thus on further disestablishment—are found in 1) profoundly contradictory moral codes (especially in the family and sexual sphere) emerging from the revolution, and 2) a significant

---

3. Andrew Greeley (1990, 24–25) introduces the concept of "loyalty" to explain the dogged disposition of some Catholics to remain faithful in the face of acknowledged disagreements with church policies and practices. Insofar as loyalty arises "because it is their birthright," loyalty is the antithesis of what we are calling personal autonomy. But insofar as loyalty leads to making "a choice to stay . . . even in the face of opposition," it is an expression of personal autonomy. Greeley, of course, is trying to understand persistence in religious observance, while we are focused on the changing meaning of that observance.

decrease in community ties. In anticipation of the analysis lying ahead, we wish here simply to identify the linkages between these two areas of change and persons' views of the church.

The New Morality

Perhaps of all aspects of the countercultural revolution that began in the 1960s, the most visible (and visibly lasting) is the emergence of an alternative moral outlook on many personal matters (Morris 1984; D'Antonio and Aldous 1983; Hunt 1974), with such diverse dimensions as women's rights, sexual norms, family authority, abortion, and single parenthood. The moral arena referred to as "the family and sexual sphere" cannot adequately be thought of as a single thing, of course. Despite this fact, however, a common theme runs through all of these dimensions (and many more on any moral agenda), and that is the notion of expanded individual *choice*. Decisions that were once the prerogative of males, or of parents, or of government, are now seen as matters of *personal, individual right*—of women to have equal access to the work force, for example, or of adult children to cohabit whether married or not.

This wholesale introduction of a new morality must be seen for what it was and is—an *alternative* definition of what is right and proper in many of life's most sensitive aspects. Behavior that was once widely regarded as deviant (even if relatively common, like divorce) was now being promulgated as a preferred, or at least legitimate, option (Yankelovich 1981). Divorce, for example, not only became more common but oftentimes no longer led to apologies by the divorcing parties; instead it was justified on mental health grounds. The rapid spread of so-called no fault divorce laws reflected exactly this remarkable increase in personal choice.

Such changes carried enormous implications for churches. Why? At the height of religion's popularity in the 1950s, little or no dissent was heard in the realm of family and sexual morality. Churches espoused the prevailing view of the intact nuclear family, and, more important, they were *seen* as upholders of this view. When the 1960s brought forth an alternative morality, therefore, churches—even though many of their leaders took forthright stands in favor of such issues as female ordination, homosexual rights, or abortion—were still regarded as bastions of the traditional values. How people felt about this new morality of radical individualism influenced their views of the church.

This radical individualism extended to religion in the form of what Roof and McKinney call the "new voluntarism." This includes not just the free choice of *how* to be religious but also the free choice of *whether* to be religious. (In Canada this free choice is documented by Bibby [1987] and in Belgium by Dobbelaere and Voyé [1990].) Among the rights being claimed by children against parents or spouse against spouse, in other words, is the right to be religious in one's own way, including the right to join a bizarre cult, meditate privately, or be altogether nonreligious.[4] There is every reason to expect a connection, therefore, between commitment to individual choice applied to religion and commitment to individual choice applied to the various dimensions of the family/sexual sphere. Rejection of the traditional code and adoption of the alternative code has as its religious parallel a shift in the view of the church from collective-expressive to individual-expressive.

Local Ties

There is a second way in which the increased personal autonomy arising out of the 1960s can be said to have jolted churches and thus contributed to a further step in the direction of disestablishment. Reference is to the greater fluidity of the population, perhaps up and down a status ladder, but certainly fluidity in geographic and social territory. The anonymity of social life has been frequently noted since World War II, as has the superficial quality of most interpersonal relationships (Bernikow 1987; Packard 1972; Perin 1988; Wireman 1984). People

---

4. Hammond (1986) shows the major increase—from 6 percent of Protestants born before World War II to 34 percent born after World War II—in the rate at which persons defected altogether from parental religion. This increase is found in all denominations for which sufficient data exist, and the pattern is found too among Catholics and Jews.

change residences as well as partners with great frequency, and any "sense of place" is honored more in nostalgia than in reality.[5] Unlike much of what is meant by "moral outlook" and a correlative sense of the right to be moral or religious in one's own way, however, this fluidity is oftentimes not a matter of individual choice—though it may be felt as "freedom" to choose—but is imposed by social circumstances. That is to say, whereas one's moral outlook may be fundamentally a matter of personality and culture, the degree to which people move, make friends, and maintain attachments to places is significantly a function of social structure—one's occupation, for example, or the age of one's children.

Evidence for this kind of change is voluminous and wide-ranging. For example, from 1960 to 1974 the percentage of American females aged 18 through 24 who were never married increased by a third. The divorce rate of women of this age during this time jumped 36 percent, and it rose 52 percent among the cohort of women a decade older (U.S. Bureau of the Census, Current Population Reports, Special Studies, Series P-23, No. 51). Fertility rates declined after the two-decade-long baby boom following World War II. From 1960 to 1978 the segment of the population living in a "family household" declined by 12 percent, while the number classified as "householder living alone" increased by 68 percent (U.S. Bureau of the Census, Current Population Reports, Series P-20). Women entered the labor force at increased rates, especially married women with husbands present.

In one sense these structural changes, which have been occurring throughout this century, were not as precipitous as the moral revolution that suddenly escalated individual choice and legitimized it with an alternative morality. But surely the latter intensified the former. For example, the ethic of personal autonomy encouraged the notion that persons have the individual right to choose their friends and decide whether to make them into lasting friendships. Hence—all else being equal—we

---

5. See, e.g., Bellah, et al. (1985, 204–06; 251, 283) for a discussion of the "yearning for small town ideals."

would expect people most committed to the alternative morality less often to form close, permanent ties, to "maintain community," than do people holding the traditional morality. But the main point to be made here is that the expansion of education, the vast increase in white-collar (and thus transferable) skills, the opportunity to upgrade housing, the freer mixing of the sexes, all led to much greater opportunities to be mobile, which in turn made maintaining community more difficult, whatever people's desire might be. So while increasing fluidity in the American population did not begin in the '60s, its impact was intensified by both cultural and structural circumstances of that period and since.

This capacity to form and keep local social ties is, like moral outlook, obviously variable. Moreover, also like moral outlook, its influence extends to churches—in this case, in the form of the differential likelihood that persons will translate local ties into parish friendships. Some people have many such friendships, others none, and most are some place in between. Partly this difference reflects individual choice, but significantly it is "built into" the situations persons cannot change but instead must adjust to. The impact is to make churches less collective-expressive and more individual-expressive.

Like an increase in moral choice, then, anything that leads to a decrease in friendship ties in churches is a jolt in the direction of further disestablishment. As Stark and Glock point out:

> A criterion of the ideal church . . . is that it function as a primary group. In turn, a criterion for the ideal church member is that he be related to his church by bonds of friendship and affection. . . . But it has been recognized that these ideals are frequently, and perhaps typically, not fulfilled either by churches or by church members in actual practice. (1968, 164)

Writing in 1967, Stark and Glock could not have known the full impact of the disestablishment jolt only then becoming manifest. They did note how the religious commitment patterns of the young were weaker than those of older persons, however, and they even conclude their volume speculating on whether that signal and others they detect in their data foretell

a "post-Christian era." A new step in the direction of disestablishment was clearly a possibility in their thinking.

The Shifting Meaning of Church

That possibility has now become an obvious reality, although
weakened religious commitment or declining church attendance rates alone are not the criterion. For one thing, not all
church attendance rates are down; some remain steady while
others actually are increasing. Another reason for withholding
judgment on implications for church attendance of the third disestablishment, however, has to do with the nature of the disestablishment jolt that has come out of the 1960s. A competing
morality and weakened community ties do not *necessarily* discourage involvement in the church. Increased personal autonomy also permits persons to choose to be *more* involved. We
shall see presently that for many people personal autonomy
does discourage involvement, but for others it does not. In this
sense the case of religion again resembles the case of ethnicity,
where the changed role played by middle-class, white ethnic
identity inhibits one kind of ethnic identity but may actually facilitate another, "voluntary" kind of ethnic identity. But a
change in the meaning of ethnicity is obviously involved. Likewise, we would contend, this new adjustment in the relationship between religion and culture must also be understood as a
change in the meaning the church has in people's lives, a
change from a collective-expressive view to an individual-
expressive view. It is thus only a first question to ask whether
increased personal autonomy has led to declining parish
involvement.

The necessary second question is whether the *meaning* of parish involvement has also changed. Evidence suggests that it
has. For example, in 1924 the Lynds found that Middletown's
church members named "habit" as their chief reason for going
to church (Lynd and Lynd 1929). It was the choice of 44 percent,
while 35 percent claimed "enjoyment," and another 8 percent
cited the benefits for their children. Thirteen percent gave other
reasons. In 1978, by contrast, Caplow and his associates report
that "habit" was selected by only 15 percent of Middletown's

church members, whereas "enjoyment" and "children's bene-fit" reasons had jumped to rates of 65 percent and 13 percent (Caplow, et al. 1983, 80). Even these latter authors, by referring to the modern reasons as "more positive," appear unwittingly to confirm the greater legitimacy accorded individuals' right to determine what the church will mean to them. Certainly it seems clear that Middletowners today feel more freedom than their predecessors of a half-century ago to make choices regard-ing their churchgoing. Caplow, et al. report no reduction in people's attachment to their own faith, but "they are reluctant to impose it on others or even to assert that it ought to be imposed" (1983, 98).

This shift from collective-expressive to individual-expressive meaning of the church is also suggested by evidence from an en-tirely different quarter: the decreasing practice of Roman Cath-olic confession. Once common, confession is now sought "at least monthly" by only 9 percent of the laity and by only 35 per-cent of clergy. John Dart, the religion writer for the *Los Angeles Times* who reported these findings (*Los Angeles Times*, February 24, 1990), quoted the U.S. bishops' study of confession practices as stating that the "variety of religious philosophies in America had eroded Catholic belief in certain church practices." Catho-lics, the study concluded, "may withhold assent and commit-ment to some individual church teaching without . . . feeling that their relationship with the church is affected in any way" (D'Antonio, et al. 1989, confirms this interpretation).[6]

Surely here is another example of the shift in the church's meaning in the individual-expressive direction. That shift, we will be arguing, is great enough to be called the third disestab-lishment.

Regional Differences in Disestablishment

One more introductory remark is in order. The next three chap-ters are designed to test the argument just advanced: that the

6. Patrick McNamara's recent (1991) study over time of successive cohorts of Catholic parochial school students uses to good advantage the framework of collective- to individual-expressive meaning to organize and understand the changes he observes.

1960s and '70s, by greatly increasing personal autonomy, have led both to the lowering of parish involvement and to a change in the meaning of such involvement. Put that way, the argument appears to be speaking of the church or churches as if what is happening in one part of the nation is happening in all, and what is happening in one denomination is happening in all. We know, however, that great regional and denominational diversity exists on the American ecclesiastical scene. The impact of the first disestablishment was no doubt felt differently on the Atlantic seaboard and on the Appalachian frontier, differently yet in the Northwest Territories. Likewise with the second disestablishment; what was a crushing blow in the Protestant Midwest may have been a welcoming embrace in Catholic New England, and perhaps hardly noticed in the Deep South.

So it is with the third disestablishment. Jolt it certainly was and is, but because what was jolted differed from one region of the United States to another, and from one denomination to another, the effects were not the same. Mainstream religion being not everywhere the same, in other words, this third step toward disestablishment has not been experienced in all regions in the same way. We will turn in chapters 5, 6, and 7, therefore, to an investigation of the "disestablishment" story in four states: Massachusetts, representing New England; Ohio, representing the Midwest; North Carolina, representing the South; and California, representing the Pacific Slope. Other states, had we researched them, would no doubt reveal somewhat different situations, but as these later chapters make clear, these four states offer plenty of contrast. Meanwhile, our first task in the next three chapters is to get some empirical grasp of the ideas just discussed.

Chapter Two

Parish Involvement
and Its Cultural Context

A Prelude

Charles Babbage, the Cambridge University mathematician, read a new poem by Tennyson containing the lines "Every minute dies a man / Every minute one is born." He thereupon wrote the poet, pointing out that the world's population was increasing, and therefore suggested that Tennyson rewrite his lines: "Every moment dies a man / And one and a sixteenth is born." Tennyson changed the poem to read: "Every moment dies a man / Every moment one is born."[1]

Poets are not alone in dismissing numbers, of course. There may indeed be some readers of this book who will proceed from this point with caution because, hereafter, numbers will be plentiful. This prelude is therefore designed to disarm such readers first by offering a justification for this quantitative analysis and second by pointing out that even when numbers are used they are used in only a few—and simple—ways.

Why are there numbers at all? For two reasons. One is that quantitative data *confirm* the argument or story line that otherwise might be told only logically, dramatically, or even poetically. More precisely, the numbers document the case by providing occasions for disconfirmatory evidence to show up; when it fails to do so, we gain confidence in the argument. From this perspective then, this study is only secondarily quantitative; the numbers are the court of last resort, so to speak.

The second reason for numbers is to aid in *discovery*. In the usual model of scientific inquiry—the experimental laboratory—numbers are used to decide whether to accept the hypothesis (with some level of confidence) because the so-called null hypothesis can be rejected. In survey research, however,

---

1. This anecdote is told in Gratzer (1989).

choices are not limited to "accept" or "reject." Because the many variables are not fixed but can be mechanically manipulated (corresponding to a repeatedly redesigned experiment), survey researchers discover things over and beyond what they were looking for. For example, in this study ethnicity was expected to play a key role in parish involvement, especially in Massachusetts. While that expectation proved false, it was "discovered" that not just ethnicity but also other institutional arrangements that presumably had enhanced parish involvement were greatly eroded in Massachusetts. This discovery fit well with the overall anticipated portrait, even though the particular role played by ethnic identity in that portrait changed.

When numbers appear here, they are used in essentially three ways only. In the majority of cases numbers appear as simple relationships between variables, generally displayed in a table or chart, which enable the reader to see that "the more X, the more Y" (or sometimes, "the more X, the more Y, depending upon conditions of Z"). In a few instances these relationships are not displayed visually but reported by a figure. The figure used here is the Pearsonian correlation coefficient (or Pearson's r), which indicates the covariation of two things and ranges hypothetically from +1.0 (X is present in exactly the ratio Y is present) through 0.0 (knowledge of X offers no indication of Y's presence) to −1.0 (X is present exactly inversely to Y's presence).

Pearson's r is involved also in the second way numbers are used here, in constructing indexes, to determine if potential items to be used in building an index are close enough to one another to be reflecting the same underlying disposition. Thus, a Pearson's r approaching ±1.0 between two items would indicate a waste of effort since item X is nearly identical with item Y. Obviously, too, a Pearson's r approaching 0.0 casts doubt on the existence of any disposition common to X and Y. From some number of interrelated items, then, those items that not only on their face seem to be measuring a common underlying dimension but also prove to be well related to one another are selected and combined into an index. This index thus measures the underlying dimension better (more reliably and validly) than does any single item. Quite a few indexes to be encountered in the following chapters were constructed in just this way.

The third numerical procedure used here is called multiple regression or path analysis, appearing only in the second part of chapter 3. This is a technique for determining the *relative* strength of the relationships between a number of presumed "causal" variables (A,B,C, etc.) and some other "caused" variable (X) when all variables are simultaneously taken into account. Thus, in chapter 3 it will be shown that, while a whole series of demographic variables have demonstrable relationships with parish involvement (and thus might be said to "cause" parish involvement), if the factors we will be calling "local ties" and "moral orientation" are entered into the analysis, these causal demographic variables for the most part cease to exert independent force. Instead, their force, we will be saying, is mediated by local ties and moral orientation.

If words can be music to poets, therefore, so can numbers be music to the mathematically inclined. The aim here, of course, is the creation of neither poetry nor mathematics but an understanding of a significant shift in religious culture in America. We are simply using numbers to aid in that endeavor. Our first task is the development of an index of parish involvement.

The Measure of Parish Involvement

It should be clear from the opening chapter that the focus of this book is on personal autonomy and the disestablishment process, not on parish involvement per se. Nonetheless, in the course of developing the empirical basis for the book's thesis, we must make use of a measure of parish involvement. Moreover, this measure must be as "generic" as possible, since we want it to be applicable to the maximum number of people. Our argument, after all, is about the considerable shift in cultural meaning that has overtaken American religious institutions in recent decades; it is involvement in those religious institutions as conventionally understood that we must therefore gauge.

In addition to a measure of involvement, we want also to explore the differing attitudinal and cultural "environments" of persons who, at one extreme, regard their parish involvement as central to their existence and, at the other extreme, have no parish identity at all.

The social scientific study of religion has long sustained a robust and, for the most part, healthy debate over the meaning and measurement of individual religiousness. From mere self-identification as Protestant, Catholic, Jew, Other, or None to elaborate multiple-dimensioned scales of "religiosity," researchers have innovated, improvised, and imitated in their desire to have a single meaningful measure. Needless to say, however, no one answer solves the problem for all purposes.[2]

The device we use here—called the Parish Involvement Index—is, we think, a particularly useful measuring tool for our purposes. We assume that people's religious lives may still be significantly patterned around parishes (churches, synagogues, mosques, etc.). We assume further that these parishes consist not only of formal organization, having membership lists, meeting times, rituals, and such, but also informal organization, occupying persons' leisure-time hours and reflecting emotional ties and symbolic importance. With these assumptions, therefore, we can inquire into the differential centrality of such parishes in the lives of those we investigate. At one extreme will be people for whom their parishes are at the core of their identities, whether primary or secondary; at the other extreme will be people entirely beyond the perimeter of the life of any parish.

The aim of the Parish Involvement Index is to classify people by their degree of "closeness to" or "involvement in" a religious organization having some kind of congregational structure. It is therefore *not* a measure of "religiousness," of "orthodoxy," or of "piety," though of course it is reasonable to assume—and we shall soon see—that this measure of involvement correlates positively with such things, since most people's religiousness, orthodoxy, etc., is typically expressed through congregational involvement. As we shall also see, however, some people regard themselves as religious even though they remain largely—even entirely—outside the orbit of ordinary church life. It is our

2. For a good review and critique of various measurement devices in this area, see Roof (1979).

purpose here to measure differential involvement in just such an orbit.

We use five pieces of information and end up with six categories of involvement. The first piece of information is a respondent's answer to the question, What is your religious preference now? (This followed the question, In what religion were you raised?) In the sample of 2,620, about 11 percent (295) said "None," and these persons constitute the category Least Involved (Score 0). The other four questions were these:

Are you a member of a church/synagogue?

Would you call yourself a strong (CURRENT PREFERENCE, as indicated in the first question) or not a very strong (CURRENT PREFERENCE)?

How often do you attend religious services?

How important would you say your particular congregation is in your life?

Persons who, having declared some kind of religious preference, and answered that they: a) belong to a church or synagogue, b) regard themselves as a strong (CURRENT PREFERENCE), c) attend at least two or three times a month, and d) report their congregation to be "very important" in their lives, constitute the Most Involved (Score 5). Persons who indicated a religious preference and gave the above answers to any three of these four questions were scored 4, those indicating a religious preference and giving any two of the above answers were scored 3, and so forth. If one imagines these five questions as "steps" toward the "center" of a congregation, then the sequence in which they are presented above would seem the logical path most people follow: they develop a preference, join, identify strongly, attend often, and regard their congregational involvement as important in their lives. Correlatively, the process of dropping out of church probably occurs in reverse order.

If everyone followed exactly this logical path, we would have what is known as a perfect Guttman scale. As it happens, 71 percent of the sample do follow this path, a fact that lends great credibility to the index, in the sense that we know both *what* it measures and that what it measures it measures *well*.

For example, elsewhere in the interview people were asked, How important would you say religion generally is in your life? The percentage answering "Very important" differs greatly according to how they are classified by their score on the index. Among those persons scoring 5 (i.e., most involved in a parish), fully 94 percent say that religion is important in their lives. The percentage drops systematically as the index score declines—to the point where, among those whose score is 0, only 17 percent report that religion is important in their lives. This relationship is portrayed graphically in the following chart.

Another observation is worth noting about this chart: Even among those scoring 0—the *least* involved in any church—17

CHART II–1

Percent saying religion "very important" increases with Parish Involvement

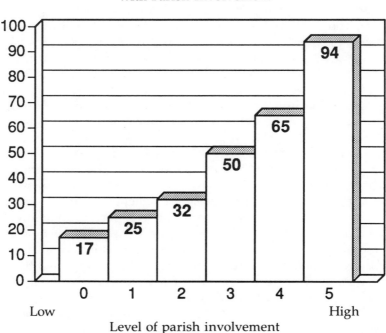

percent report that religion is nonetheless "very important" in their lives. We shall have occasion later to identify people of this sort—religious souls, perhaps, but isolated, at least from religion's conventional structures.

The Meaning of the Parish Involvement Index

One can object to our index on the grounds that, by giving centrality to the parish, we are measuring conventional religious expression but not its unconventional counterparts. What about people who take their religion via television? Or who read devotions and/or theology at home? Or who rely on Dial-a-Prayer for daily guidance? It is correct to say that such persons would not score high on our index (unless they also met our criteria). Moreover, it is no doubt wise to remember that there are many ways of being religious without being conventionally religious.

Nonetheless, two justifications can be offered for using a measure like the Parish Involvement Index *in our investigation.* One is the fact that our interest (and that of the Lilly Endowment, the sponsor of our research) is precisely in so-called mainstream (i.e., conventional) religion. We are not *un*interested in unconventional expressions of religion—in due course we shall encounter some in this book—but our major interest is in conventional religious organizations because of what we think has been happening to them, and we are using randomly sampled individuals in four states as our informants. We are less interested in *how* they are religious, in other words, and more interested in *the degree to which they utilize conventional parish structures to be religious.* One will note, for example, that the information we use in scoring people with this index is not biased in any direction except toward conventionality. Respondents can be Protestants, Catholics, or Jews, Liberal or Conservative, Pentecostal or liturgical, attend country church or city cathedral; all have equal chance of scoring low-to-high on our index. It is true that if people are religious in some manner that involves no congregation and no religious services, then they could not score high on our index. On the other hand, given the nature of contemporary American society, are not such people reasonably regarded as religiously unconventional?

The second justification is found in the revealing correlates of the Parish Involvement Index. As we will now begin to show, these are many and strong. Our index is powerful in its meaning; it indicates a good deal about the differing cultural contexts of persons who score at its several levels. We begin, in Table II–1, with the relationship between parish involvement and other religious characteristics.

The 8 lines of Table II–1 reveal the vividly different religious worlds in which our respondents live. We will take the time

Table II–1
Parish Involvement and a Number of
Other Religious Characteristics

| | Parish Involvement Score | | | | | |
| | Low | | | | | High |
Background Characteristics	0	1	2	3	4	5
1. % Attended church weekly as a child	81	83	86	85	85	87
2. % Attended church weekly as a young adult	14	20	27	38	48	64
Pious Practices/Beliefs						
3. % Pray daily	19	34	45	64	75	90
4. % Read Bible at home	30	44	53	64	74	89
5. % Usually say grace at meals	12	16	27	41	48	71
6. % Bible to be understood literally	15	38	36	41	52	64
7. % Believe in eternal life	52	77	82	89	92	96
8. % Believe in the devil	28	56	58	71	78	84
No. of Cases*	(295)	(456)	(472)	(383)	(422)	(588)

*Number of cases varies since not everybody answered every question.

here simply to highlight two generalizations based on these remarkably strong relationships:

Lines 1–2. Finding: No significant difference exists in the childhood exposure to church attendance between the currently uninvolved and currently very involved, though differential involvement appears well established by young adulthood.

Lines 3–8. Finding: Parish involvement is strongly related to pious or "orthodox" ritual practices and beliefs.

While there are no surprises in Table II–1 (indeed, had any of these relationships been reversed, we would have had cause for questioning the meaning of our index), there is ample evidence that the Parish Involvement Index measures a broadly meaningful distinction among individuals. As we set about to analyze these data further and explore both reasons for and consequences of differences in this index, we can note the significance of line 1: These differences are not merely inherited from childhood. Therefore, it seems reasonable to conclude that the differences in parish involvement develop after childhood, although they are firmly evident by young adulthood. Furthermore, lines 3–8 tell us that our measure of parish involvement also reflects a wider scope of "conventional" religiousness, from daily prayer to belief in the devil.

We seem to have grasped a wide-ranging and pervasive religious difference among individuals. Without claiming that those persons scoring low on the Parish Involvement Index are therefore areligious, let alone antireligious (a quarter of them, after all, report praying daily; a third engage in home Bible reading; over half believe in eternal life), we do feel safe in claiming to have measured a significant dimension of these people's religious lives: the centrality of their congregational involvement. The implications for whatever comprises "mainstream" religion are thus clear. Ranging from nonexistent to very high indeed, this measure also tells us a lot about other aspects of respondents' religious orientation. It is not surprising, therefore, to discover its relationship to denomination.

We will follow the strategy employed in Roof and McKinney's *American Mainline Religion* (1987), not just classifying people as Protestant, Catholic, or Jew but further categorizing Protestants into "families" of Liberal, Moderate, Conservative, and Black, giving separate denominational rates where we can, even if few members are represented. Our families are not identical with Roof and McKinney's, but the resemblance is great. As can readily be seen, denominations and families of denominations differ considerably in their rates of highly involved members, defined as those scoring 4 and 5 on the Index of Parish Involvement.

There are no real surprises in this table either. The comparative rates of high parish involvement for the several families of denominations and for separate denominations for which we have adequate cases are probably expected. Roman Catholics fall in the middle, between Liberal/Moderate Protestants on the one hand, and Conservative Protestants on the other hand. Among Conservative Protestants, Free Will Baptists and Holiness members have unusually low rates of highly involved persons and Seventh-Day Adventists an unusually high rate (though it should be noted that these percentages are based on relatively few cases). Similarly, those identifying themselves as American Baptist have a surprisingly high rate compared with other Moderate Protestants (though again the number of cases is only 8). Jews and Unitarian/Universalists report the lowest rates of highly involved parishioners, and—as would be expected from the results of other studies—such groups as Jehovah's Witnesses, Seventh-Day Adventists, and Mormons exhibit quite high rates. So do Black Protestants.

In sum, the Parish Involvement Index appears to reflect the real situation we would expect.

Parish Involvement and Social Ties

Table II–1 showed that the Index of Parish Involvement is associated with the considerably different religious worlds people live in. It is reasonable to surmise that their social worlds, their cultural surroundings, differ in other ways as well—that they dwell, for example, in different kinds of friendship networks. Table II–3 tells us a good deal about these social worlds. The relationships it reports are arranged in descending order; that is, the items at the top of the table are items with which differential

Table II–2
Rates of High Involvement in Various Denominations

Denomination	% Highly Involved	Total No. of Cases
Roman Catholic	46	699
Jewish	10	49
Liberal Protestant	30	210
United Church of Christ	19	42
Episcopal	38	53
Presbyterian	34	102
Unitarian/Universalist	8	13
Moderate Protestant	37	327
American Baptist	63	8
Disciples	30	23
Lutheran (excluding Missouri Synod)	39	88
Methodist	37	208
Conservative Protestant	49	726
Assemblies of God	69	16
Baptist, nonspecific	47	216
Free Will Baptist	39	33
Holiness	33	12
Jehovah's Witnesses	54	13
Mormon	71	24
"Other" Protestant	59	111
Pentecostal	56	48
Seventh-Day Adventist	80	10
Southern Baptist	56	137
Nondenominational*	29	106
Black Protestant	63	168

*Even with dozens of coding options and instructions to probe, interviewers end up often with answers not readily codable. "Nondenominational," for example, surely includes many fundamentalists who, on principle, will not see their churches "yoked" with others. But the low rate (30%) of Highly Involved among these people must just as surely mean that this category involves a variety of nonfundamentalists as well—perhaps suburban "community church" members. The "Other" Protestant category is equally vague, and with an involvement rate twice that of the Nondenominationals, chances are good that the two groups of respondents are differently situated.

parish involvement is strongly related, while items at the bottom of the table deal with social networks seemingly unrelated to parish involvement. It is important to remember, of course, that the *absolute* rate at which people answer questions is a function of how the questions are worded. This makes for dubious comparisons between questions, so it is not the absolute rate but the *relative* rate we look at. How do persons with different parish involvement scores differ in the way they answer these questions?

The first few lines indicate what we would expect of people who differ in parish involvement: Those most involved have more friends at church (lines 1, 5), they are more likely to be surrounded by religiously like-minded persons at home (line 3) and elsewhere (line 4), and they count more churchgoers among their acquaintances (line 2). These findings are not remarkable.

It is in lines 6 through 10 that we begin to see how parish involvement is linked to wider social networks. Thus, from line 6 we learn that the highly involved are more likely to be integrated into their neighborhoods, and from line 9 we learn something similar—that their friendship networks are more local than the friendship networks of the less involved. But note, too, that similar relationships are found with respect to involvement in the wider kin group (line 7), with fellow ethnics (line 8), and even modestly with fellow workers (line 10).

Two other questions, not shown in Table II–3, show finally that some social networks remain unrelated to parish involvement. No differences exist between those high and low in parish involvement in their likelihood of a) belonging to one or more voluntary associations (about one-third at each score level belong) or b) maintaining close friendships with at least a few former schoolmates (about 55 percent at each score level do).

We are reminded by all ten of the items in Table II–3, nonetheless, how "social" an activity parish involvement can be, how far-ranging this sociability can be, and how much, therefore, parish involvement may be not only a *source* of sociability (as is suggested by the presentation of the data in Table II–3) but a *response* to sociability as well (as we will discuss in the next chapter). That is to say, church involvement may flow out of

Table II–3

Parish Involvement and Social Network Characteristics

% Who Report:	Low					High
	0	1	2	3	4	5
1. Feeling very close to many people at church/synagogue	*	4	12	20	33	66
2. Most of their friends attend church/synagogue regularly	21	29	37	54	66	78
3. Most of their family members share their religious views	57	63	71	80	85	89
4. Most of their other everyday contacts share their religious views	37	50	54	59	61	66
5. Most of their really close friends attend the same church/synagogue	*	5	7	12	17	35
6. Being close to at least a few people in their neighborhood	48	53	58	62	65	75
7. Being close to many relatives outside of their immediate family	31	30	36	41	44	55
8. Most of their really close friends share their ethnic background	49	55	61	58	66	67
9. Most of their really close friends live in their local area	42	40	45	44	48	59
10. Being close to at least a few people they work with	74	81	75	80	86	85
No. of Cases**	(295)	(456)	(472)	(383)	(422)	(588)

*Persons with a score of 0 on the Parish Involvement Index were not asked these questions.
**Number of cases varies since not everybody was asked every question.

collective ties and be expressive of them as well as encourage and help maintain them.

At the same time it is just as clear that high parish involvement is not synonymous with this kind of sociability. After all, one-third of those scoring 5 on the Parish Involvement Index do *not* feel close to many others at their church or synagogue (line 1), and two-thirds report that most of their really close friends are found elsewhere than at their church (line 5). As for all the other indications of social relationships, it is obvious that while they are correlated with parish involvement, they are generally less strongly associated with it. And what *this* says to us is that, if the church expresses membership in social collectivities for some people, it appears not to do so for others. For these latter, the church is individual-expressive, to use the terms from chapter 1.

Parish Involvement and the Moral World

It is not just in their social worlds, their friendship networks and ties with others, that people differing in parish involvement differ from each other. They also differ in the moral worlds they inhabit, in their views of what is right and wrong. Our investigation in one sense, then, confirms what we have known all along: that churchgoing implies the likelihood of holding certain moral positions not shared by nonchurchgoers.

What comes as a surprise in Table II–4, therefore, is learning the shape and content of these moral differences. Where difference might have been expected, it is not found; and where it might have been thought unlikely, it turns out to be profoundly related to parish involvement.

Table II–4 requires careful study. If one started by observing lines 5 and 6, one might be tempted to think of parish involvement as a surrogate measure of moral "confinement." That is, high involvement is associated with rigid obedience to law, while lower levels of involvement carry ever more relaxed or qualified understanding of what the law requires. No one, for example, would argue that cheating on taxes or insurrection is *never* wrong rather than *always* wrong. Instead, the argument would be over the conditions permitting actions, normally

Table II–4
Parish Involvement and Moral Outlook Characteristics

	Parish Involvement Score					
	Low					High
% Who State:	0	1	2	3	4	5
1. Premarital sex is always wrong	11	17	19	34	42	63
2. Homosexual relations are always wrong	44	54	61	68	71	84
3. Abortion is always wrong	14	16	20	27	39	52
4. The husband ought to have the main say-so in family matters	13	20	22	26	33	47
5. Cheating on taxes is always wrong	58	61	66	69	72	86
6. Overthrowing the government is always wrong	42	47	50	53	56	58
7. The rules about morality preached by churches/ synagogues are just too restrictive	57	45	38	31	22	14
No. of Cases*	(295)	(456)	(472)	(383)	(422)	(588)

*Number of cases varies since not everybody answered every question.

wrong, to be acceptable. Such an interpretation of lines 5 and 6 suggests that parish involvement is related to an "absolutist" moral perspective, with nonchurchgoers reflecting more and more the perspective of "situation ethics." This interpretation also provides meaning to line 7, where parish involvement is seen to be associated *inversely* with agreement that the church's moral rules are too restrictive and should allow for conditional approval of some erstwhile forbidden actions.

But above lines 5 and 6 are four items that ask about behaviors some people take "always" to be wrong while others take "never" to be wrong. That is to say, a number of respondents—and the proportion goes up as the level of parish involvement goes down—are not satisfied with answering that premarital sex, homosexuality, abortion, and domestic equality *may* be all right under some conditions, but they go further and say they are *never* wrong. In the case of lines 1, 2, and 3, even though in the telephone interview respondents were provided only the options of answering "always," "usually," or "only sometimes" wrong, a surprising 13 percent, 9 percent, and 7 percent volunteered answers to these three questions that those actions are "never" wrong. In the case of line 4, fully 71 percent *dis*agreed that husbands should hold unequal power in the household.

What we observe, then, is not simply an association between parish involvement and moral absolutism but between parish involvement and fundamental disagreement over the morality underlying the conventional ethics of the pre-1960s. If this interpretation is correct—and later analysis will tend to be confirming—then line 7 can be understood as not simply a call for more flexibility in the churches' moral code but a challenge to replace it. At least on certain issues. Given the fact that lines 1–4 of Table II–4 are among the more robust correlations observed in this chapter means that parish involvement is importantly related to concurrence in the conventional ethics now being challenged, as well as the view, no doubt, that churches and synagogues ought to be custodians of those conventional ethics.

Just how pointed this relationship is can be demonstrated by referring to a number of moral issues showing little or no correlation with parish involvement. For example, the most involved (Score 5), when compared with the least involved (Score 0), were only 10 percentage points less inclined to spend more government money on welfare (31 percent vs. 41 percent). They were only 6 percentage points less inclined to spend more on the environment (88 percent vs. 95 percent), and showed no significant difference on the issue of whether labor unions have too much power (60 percent vs. 60 percent) or the issue of opposing

the death penalty (24 percent vs. 22 percent). Only with the issue of the government's spending less on defense does high
parish involvement (49 percent approval of lower spending) di-
verge from low parish involvement (70 percent approval) to the
degree it did on tax-cheating and insurrection. And none of
these issues exhibits the magnitude of difference shown in lines
1–4 of Table II–4—all in the realm of family and sexual ethics.

As with the set of social network items, one can ask
whether—as the data presentation of Table II–4 would suggest—parish involvement leads to habitation in a conventional
moral world or whether the reverse is true. Is a conventional
moral outlook, especially in the family/sexual sphere, a *response*
to parish involvement or a *source* of it? Like the sociability issue
also, we must wait until the next chapter to address this difficult
question.

Before moving to a new chapter, however, we have one more
bit of analysis of parish involvement to perform.

The Dynamics of Parish Involvement

The portrait of parish involvement just painted is by no means
static. Involvement obviously waxes and wanes throughout persons' lives, as many studies have shown (e.g., Hoge and Roozen
1979). While we asked questions of our respondents at only one
point in time, we did include the query, Would you say you are
more involved in a church/synagogue now than you were five
years ago? Or would you say less involved, or about the same?
Approximately half answered "about the same," and this proportion held for almost all the denominational families. (The exceptions: Black Protestants, of whom only 27 percent gave this
answer, and the Nones [Score 0 on the index] of whom 61 percent gave this answer.)

What about the other half—those who answered they are
now "more involved" or "less involved" than five years ago?
The answer is that Roman Catholics who changed from five
years ago are split exactly in half between those more and those
less involved now than five years ago. White Protestants appear
net losers, with about 60 percent of the Liberals decreasing as 40
percent have increased. Moderate Protestants suffer somewhat

less, with a 54–46 percentage break, while Conservative Protestants lose at the rate of 56 to 44 percent. Jews have a similar record (54 percent "less," 46 percent "more"), though the cases are few. Only the Other Religions and Black Protestants have enjoyed a net gain from changers during the past five years (though in the case of Other Religions, their 58–42 gain is based on only 19 cases). Black Protestants' gain was 55 as compared with a 45 percent loss. As might be expected, among the current Nones, all who reported changing reported less involvement.

As might also be expected, reports of greater involvement now than five years ago tend to come overwhelmingly from persons now scoring 4 or 5 on the Parish Involvement Index, while reports of lesser involvement tend to come from persons scoring 1 or 2 (and to a lesser extent 3) on this index. In principle, of course, we might have discovered, especially at one or both extremes of the Parish Involvement Index, considerable stability, but only the Nones approximate this situation. As we saw, however, 39 percent have reached their 0 score by decreasing from some higher level of involvement within the past five years.

The implication is that instead of considerable stability we observe considerable fluidity, up and down the scale, and at all points on the scale. It is true that a net erosion over the past five years seems to have taken place—at 53–47 = 6 percent if the current Nones are excluded from the calculation (or at 57–43 = 14 percent if they are included). This erosion is not good news from the standpoint of churches, needless to say, but on the other hand little more than half of the changing is downward; almost half is upward.

From our perspective, the point is that the parish involvement situation is quite fluid and thus subject to social forces that influence it. We turn in the next chapter to an investigation of some of these forces.

Chapter Three

Sources of
Parish Involvement

In the previous chapter we learned quite a lot about the characteristics accompanying differential parish involvement. If we are to understand more about the reasons for differing levels of conventional religious behavior, however, we must seek not just correlates of such behavior but its sources. That is our aim in this chapter.

In addition to a variety of demographic factors (e.g., gender, age, marital status, socioeconomic status)—many of which we will encounter presently—studies of American churchgoing in recent decades have consistently found two quite different sources of differential involvement, reviewed in the opening chapter and indirectly addressed in chapter 2. One of these sources is eminently social structural and reflects the degree to which people are linked to their local surroundings. Because congregations (as we use the term here) are always local to some territory, it is understandable that people who regard themselves as tied to that local territory will tend also to be involved in one or another of its parish congregations. Research has shown, moreover, that mere length of residence in an area does not, in and of itself, lead to greater organizational involvement. Only insofar as length of residence facilitates social linkages does it seem to encourage such involvement (Welch 1983; Welch and Baltzell 1984; Kasarda and Janowitz 1974). This source of involvement is sometimes called the "belonging" source.

The other source of differential parish involvement is cultural, not social structural. Where the effect of local territorial ties is thought to operate somewhat independently of the attitudes, beliefs, or values of the persons comprising those ties, the effect of the cultural factor depends upon persons' viewpoints.

The first source is more "Durkheimian" in that it assumes that the church expresses or represents a social group; people will therefore be involved to the extent they are part of that group. The church for them is a way of belonging, an "agency" of their social identity. In chapter 1 we called this the collective-expressive view. The second source—sometimes referred to as the "meaning" source—is more "Weberian" in that it assumes that the church is one way by which people may try to make sense out of life. Persons will be involved to the extent their church's viewpoint makes meaningful their own. The church for these people serves a private purpose. We called this the individual-expressive view in chapter 1. For some persons, of course, the church may be a source of both belonging and also of meaning. We look now at two measures designed to capture these two sources of differential involvement. (McGuire 1987, ch. 2, offers an excellent review of these two perspectives.)

The Local Ties Index

Our first aim is to classify people by their degree of embedded-ness in a local community. Do people's friendship ties indicate a strong social connection to their local area? Not necessarily. In contemporary society it is increasingly easy for friendship ties to transcend local boundaries and/or to be of a "secondary" instead of a "primary" nature. Indeed, in chapter 1 we presented a variety of evidence to suggest that—through such channels as geographic mobility, delayed marriage, divorce, educational mobility, and female participation in the labor force—especially since the 1960s people are increasingly "unbound" to local territory. That is to say, many persons may really be acquaintances rather than friends of those living nearby. In the extreme, they may even be strangers in their own neighborhoods. It was our intent to identify people who have primary relationships with others in their immediate social surroundings, and that led to the Local Ties Index.

We use two items from the survey to measure the extent of these local ties. On the first item, respondents were told to "think about people you feel really close to—people you could confide in." Then they were asked, How about people who live in your neighborhood? Are you close to many of them, a few of them, or hardly any of them? On the second item respondents were asked to "think of *all* your really close friends—relatives, co-workers, friends from school, and church, and so forth." Then, how many of them live right in your local area—nearly all of them, most of them, or only a few of them? On both of these items a number of respondents volunteered a "none" answer. The "hardly any" and "none" categories of the first item were collapsed, as were the "nearly all" and "most" categories of the second item. The two items were then crosstabulated, yielding the following distribution of cases:

ITEM 2
How Many of One's Close Friends Live in Local Area

ITEM 1		Nearly all or most	Only a few	None
Close to how	*Many*	326	146	10
many in one's	*A few*	546	524	54
neighborhood	*Hardly any or none*	356	499	141

2,602

It can be noted that answers to these two questions are positively correlated, but they are not identical in their meaning. Therefore, as was discussed in chapter 2 (and is discussed again in Appendix B, "The Research Process"), one criterion of a good index is met in that both questions reflect a single underlying dimension, but each reflects that dimension distinctively. One clue to this distinctiveness is found by comparing the lower left-hand corner (with 356 cases) with the upper right-hand corner (with only 10 cases). This comparison makes clear that there are many whose close friends live in the local area though hardly any neighbors are close friends, while the reverse is a rare situation—reporting that none of one's close friends live in the local area but nonetheless feeling close to many in the neighborhood. Had the opposite pattern been found, we would have reason to believe that respondents either misunderstood the questions or answered randomly. As it is, we have two probes that tell us in two different ways how embedded people are in their local communities.

Persons who answered that they a) feel close to many people who live in their neighborhood and b) indicate that nearly all or most of their close friends live in their local area (upper left corner) constitute the category Strong Local Ties (Score 4 on the index). Conversely, persons who feel close to hardly any or none of their neighbors and who indicate that none of their close friends live in their local area (lower right corner) constitute the category Weak Local Ties (Score 0 on the index). Diagonal lines in the above diagram show how cells were combined to make the categories with scores of 3, 2, and 1 on the index. The frequency distribution for this index is as follows:

Local Ties Index

Index	Score	Frequency	Percent
0	Weak	141	5
1		553	21
2		890	34
3		692	27
4	Strong	326	13
	Total	2,602	100

The two items comprising the Local Ties Index will be recognized as lines 1 and 5 of Table II–3 in the previous chapter. There we showed that parish involvement is correlated with having local friends; now we have turned the order around, combined two items dealing with local friends, and we will soon report that the resulting index measures one *source* of parish involvement. Is that justified, since we already know the positive correlations?

The answer is Yes because, as will be seen later in this chapter, we are not using the word "source" to mean ultimate source or first cause. Before persons can be highly involved members of a parish, for example, they must be born, so one might think of birth as, in this sense, the ultimate source or cause of parish involvement. But such thinking is recognized to be off base not because it is false but because it is not the answer to the question we are really asking. Or, to put it differently, we are not so much interested in what *causes* parish involvement as we are in understanding *how it comes about*. What are its dynamics, the forces that influence it up or down? As we will be saying repeatedly in this chapter, embeddedness in a local community will be seen to enhance parish involvement, but so—it seems reasonable to assume—does parish involvement enhance embeddedness in a local community. It is enough to know that they covary. That makes local ties a "source" for our purposes. Moreover, once we introduce a number of demographic variables, the issue of what is cause and what is effect will evaporate as an issue.

Two other items on the survey are useful in helping us establish the meaning of the index, therefore giving us confidence that it does, as we claim, measure the extent of people's local ties. The survey asked; If you could live anywhere you wanted, where would you live? Line 1 of Table III–1 shows responses to this question, crosstabulated by the Local Ties Index. If our index measures the degree of embeddedness in a local community, we would certainly expect it to be related to people's desire to remain in their particular community, even if given the chance to relocate. In fact, as we move from the weak end of the index to the strong end, people's preference for living in the community where they currently reside increases sharply.

We get additional evidence of the index's validity from answers to another item in the survey, shown in line 2 of this table. It assesses the density of people's friendship networks by probing as follows: "Now think of *all* your really close friends—relatives, co-workers, friends from school and church, and so forth. How many of *them* know *each other*—nearly all of them, most of them, or only a few of them?" The table shows that our index is strongly correlated with this friendship network item, suggesting that people who score high on local ties are, in fact, embedded in a local community environment.

It is clear then that as the score on the Local Ties Index increases, so does the likelihood that persons' networks of friends become more circumscribed. Not only are their intimate friends

Table III–1

Living Preference and Friendship Network by Local Ties

	Local Ties Index				
	Weak				Strong
	0	1	2	3	4
1. Percent preferring to live in the same community	28	39	47	56	61
2. Percent indicating that "nearly all" or "most" of their friends know each other	32	35	45	64	77
No. of Cases	141	553	890	692	326

more likely to be close by, thus making the local community more attractive, but so also are these friends more likely to know each other. We have thus a good measure of the degree to which people are embedded in their local communities.

As anticipated at the outset of this chapter, the higher the score on this measure, the higher the score on the Parish Involvement Index. Thirty-nine percent of those most embedded in neighborhood friendships are high (Score 5) in parish involvement, and this percentage declines steadily to 13 percent of those least embedded. This relationship is, of course, the one expected *to the degree church involvement reflects group membership* and is not simply a matter of individual choice. It is the "Durkheimian" or "belonging" view of religion—that churches express, convey, and help maintain the important collectivities of which people are part. The following chart is a vivid representation of this view.

Morality and the Churches

The second source of differential parish involvement we wish to explore is not structural but cultural. It is the church as individual-expressive rather than collective-expressive. It reflects the fact that churches may play a symbolic role—a

CHART III–1
Percent scoring high in Parish Involvement increases with local ties

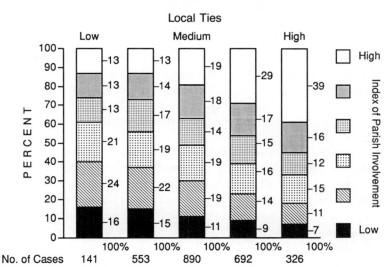

Local Ties

meaning-providing role—that transcends their theological identities. It is hardly surprising that persons who hold a literal interpretation of the Bible, for example, will more likely be found in a parish that likewise regards the Bible as literally true. But beyond their biblical positions, and in addition to a range of other doctrinal matters, churches symbolize a number of matters that by no means are dictated by their doctrine but nonetheless are attached to them by public perception, thus allowing more individual choice to come into play.

Many community studies, for example, show an obvious social class basis to denominations; people presumably choose their affiliation, and their degree of involvement, by the "closeness of fit" between a church's prestige and their real (or hoped-for) social standing. The character and quality of a church's music may be another cultural consideration, as might its youth ministry or its programs for the elderly. Where local ties and church friendships may in some sense "dictate" parish involvement, therefore, the kinds of cultural factors we have in mind here are far more voluntary; people search out and "match" their own tastes with those of a church.

The point, however, is not to elaborate all possible roles a church may play but to identify one particular role it plays now, toward the end of the twentieth century. We refer to the church as symbol of moral conventionality. We have good grounds for concentrating on moral conventionality because of the strong correlations uncovered in the previous chapter (Table II–4) regarding parish involvement and moral outlook in the family/sexual sphere.

Since the 1960s there has been widespread challenge to what was conventional before that. Assaults on the success ethic, for example, have had ramifications in the workplace, and demands for gender equality have had remarkable impact on the entry of women into the voluntary labor force. Demands for equal civil rights have accompanied expanded notions of civil liberties. Old-fashioned patriotism has been challenged, just as partisan politics have undergone shifts and realignments. The 1960s truly gave rise to a "counter" culture, the reverberations of which are still strongly felt (see Yankelovich 1974, 1981). But nowhere has the challenge been greater than in the sphere of family life and sexual *mores*. And churches, we have seen, whether or not they sought the role, have been cast as custodians of the earlier "traditional" morality. Despite public pronouncements by some church leaders—especially from the Liberal family of Protestant denominations but also from some Moderate denominations, Roman Catholic bishops, and Jewish leaders—churches appear to the public to be overwhelmingly associated not with the new but with the old moral positions regarding family and sexual matters.

In the case of Conservative denominations the situation would appear simple to understand: Conservative leaders express the traditional outlook, constituents are largely in agreement with that outlook, and—to the degree the morality issue plays a role in parish involvement—those parishioners most in agreement are most involved. But why would much this same picture be duplicated in denominations whose leaders are outspoken advocates of a changing morality? The answer, at a broad level at least, has to be that churches of all kinds (including synagogues) remain symbols of conventionality; whoever feels most comfortable with society's conventions feels most comfortable in church—assuming, of course, that all other factors are constant. We can make this argument more clearly after introducing another index.

The Morality Index

Believing that for religious organizations this realm of family and sexual mores is the most central of the various challenges to traditional morality, we asked several questions in the survey designed to measure people's views in this realm. We have met them already as lines 1–4 of Table II–4. Three of the questions read as follows:

Do you believe that sexual relations before marriage are *always* morally wrong, *usually* morally wrong, or only *sometimes* morally wrong?

How about homosexual relations? Are they *always* morally wrong, *usually* morally wrong, or only *sometimes* morally wrong?

How about abortion? Is it *always* morally wrong, *usually* morally wrong, or only *sometimes* morally wrong?

A number of respondents rejected all of these choices and volunteered that one or more of these activities are *never* wrong. The fourth question asked respondents to agree or disagree with the statement:

Some equality in marriage is a good thing, but by and large the husband ought to have the main say-so in family matters.

If on the first item—sex before marriage—respondents indicated that such behavior is *always* morally wrong, they were given a score of 1 for that item. If people responded by indicating that the behavior is either *usually* morally wrong or *only sometimes* morally wrong, they received a score of 0. A volunteered *never* morally wrong response was given a −1 score for that item. The second and third items—homosexuality and abortion—were coded in the same manner. For the final item on marital equality, agreeing with the statement earned respondents a score of 1, disagreeing a score of −1, and no response at all was coded as 0. The scores for all four items were then summed for each respondent, giving us a new variable we call the Morality Index. Scores on the index vary from −4 to 4. The frequency distribution of the index is presented below.

	Morality Index		
	Index Score	Frequency	Percent
Alternative morality	−4	60	2
	−3	104	4
	−2	142	5
	−1	587	22
	0	514	20
	1	377	14
	2	348	13
Traditional morality	3	223	9
	4	265	10
	Total	2,620	99

We have good empirical reasons for believing that these items fit well together and constitute a valid measure of a traditional vs. an alternative moral outlook. First, we analyzed these four items along with ten other morality items (relating to the role of women in society, libertarian values, the death penalty, etc.) to get a sense of how, statistically, they fit together. This process is called a factor analysis and is designed to reveal which items are most strongly related to each other. Those having the greatest coherence emerge as Factor #1, those with the next greatest coherence as Factor #2, etc. It turns out that the items which emerge as dominant in Factor #1 in the analysis are precisely those items which we use here as indicators of alternative vs. traditional morality—abortion, homosexuality, premarital sex, and equality in marriage. We know therefore that these four variables are strongly and positively related to each other. If they were not related in this way, we would have no basis for arguing that they are measuring the same underlying thing—moral outlook in the family/sexual sphere—but in fact the inter-item correlations range from .288 to .510 and all are statistically very significant.

Second, if our index is a valid measure of moral outlook, ranging from a traditional orientation to an alternative morality, we would expect it to be strongly related to the survey item which asks people to locate themselves on a Liberal to Conservative continuum. In fact, as the chart below illustrates, the relationship is strong and in the expected direction.

It is obvious that, as one moves from −4 (alternative morality) to +4 (traditional morality), the proportion of Liberals systematically declines and the proportion of Conservatives systematically increases. As another indication, people scored here as most traditional reported support for Bush over Dukakis by more than two to one; those scored as least traditional supported Dukakis over Bush by more than two to one. (Most of the interviews were conducted in October 1988; many interviews in Ohio occurred after the election, and the question was changed to "voted for" rather than "support.")

This relationship between moral outlook in the family/sexual sphere and self-identification as Liberal or Conservative (or direction of presidential vote) is, of course, to be expected. It is important to the analysis here, moreover, that our measure of alternative vs. traditional morality be seen for the powerful index it is of Americans' overall division along value lines. The next table provides some evidence by showing how people's scores on the Morality Index are reflected in a variety of value areas.

Line 1 of Table III–2 is close to a tautology, of course, because one of the four items in the Morality Index asked about equality between husbands and wives, and the question reflected in line 1 is really an extension of this issue. It is perhaps worth noting that nearly two-thirds of even the most traditional moralists agree that outside jobs are good for women. Even stronger support is expressed by all others.

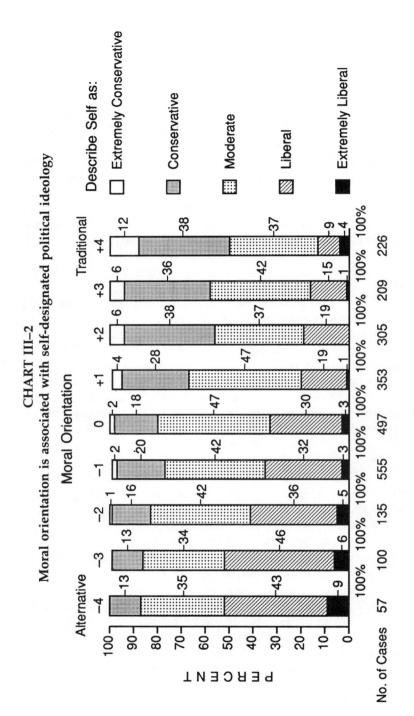

CHART III-2

Moral orientation is associated with self-designated political ideology

Table III–2
The Morality Index and Other Value Positions

	Morality Index								
	Alternative				0	Traditional			
% Who Agree That:	−4	−3	−2	−1	0	+1	+2	+3	+4
1. Jobs outside the home are good for women	85	94	94	90	91	81	81	72	60
2. Women should be eligible for ordination	100	99	97	95	89	80	69	56	51
3. Government should spend less on defense	78	73	72	66	54	54	50	48	42
4. Government should spend more on the environment	93	95	95	93	92	90	88	88	85
5. Cheating on taxes is always wrong	50	48	56	62	65	73	80	83	91
6. Overthrowing the government is always wrong	25	36	37	42	56	58	57	52	70
No. of Cases*	(60)	(104)	(142)	(587)	(514)	(377)	(348)	(223)	(265)

*Number of cases varies since not everybody answered every question.

A similar pattern is found in line 2, which asks about women's ordination. It is remarkable that 100 percent of those on the extreme left on this scale support such action, and that such support steadily declines as one moves toward the traditional end of the continuum, but, even so, half of even the most traditional respondents now support the ordaining of women. Like the voluntary entry of women into the labor market in recent decades, women's ordination has gone from the nearly unthinkable to the clearly accepted—though not equally by all.

The next two items (lines 3 and 4) ask about current government expenditures: Should there be less on defense and more on the environment? Clearly the Morality Index differentiates among people on these two issues; traditionalists are less willing to cut back on defense spending, though they are nearly as willing to see more spent on the environment. Again, events and movements in America (and elsewhere) since the 1960s are reflected in these answers.

Lines 5 and 6 differentiate the new moralists from the traditionalists somewhat more sharply. The new moralists are considerably more likely to entertain the idea that cheating on taxes and even the idea of insurrection may sometimes be permitted. Our questionnaire did not allow for people to stipulate the conditions under which they would approve of these acts, but the pattern of answers nevertheless makes clear that the alternative morality (perhaps "situation ethics" is a suitable synonym here) allows for greater flexibility on the moral scene. It will come as no shock, therefore, to see—as we have seen indirectly already in Table II–4 and as we will see again presently—how strongly related is the Morality Index with parish involvement.

Morality and Parish Involvement

In light of our discussion prior to introducing the Morality Index—a discussion to the effect that churches and synagogues are apparently regarded as institutions of conventionality—it is to be expected that persons' moral outlook influences their involvement in parishes. Let us look first at this relationship, contained in the next chart.

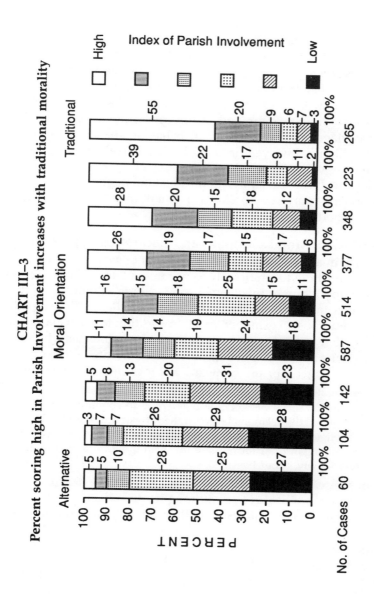

CHART III-3

Percent scoring high in Parish Involvement increases with traditional morality

The strong relationship morality has with parish involvement is seen in this chart; it is powerful (Pearson's r = .417). Nothing in our survey has the explanatory power of this Morality Index, though it, like the Local Ties Index, may be as much "caused" by parish involvement as "causing" it. But whatever the reason, persons strongly committed to the conventional rules relating to marriage, family, and sexual behavior are far more likely to be highly involved in parish life; correlatively, persons strongly favoring new rules in this area of life are far less likely to be involved. Certainly moral position in the family/sexual sphere is a source of parish involvement in the sense "source" is used here.

Local Ties, Moral Outlook, and Local–Cosmopolitanism

In 1978, in a book entitled *Community and Commitment*, W. Clark Roof contributed significantly to our understanding of religious belief and church involvement by calling attention to the revelance in parish studies of the factor he called, following others, "locals" vs. "cosmopolitans." In addition to the usual social factors that facilitate or inhibit individual religiousness, he said, there is the matter of whether persons are oriented more toward their local circles or more toward wider circles. He later wrote:

> For "locals," i.e., those persons who are most involved in local community social networks and oriented to community norms and values, the relations between the infrastructure and subjective religiosity should be stronger than would be the case for "cosmopolitans," or those more involved in and oriented to the larger society. (Roof 1988a, 308)

Roof's research, and that of subsequent others, demonstrated the correctness of this line of thought.

Roof measured local–cosmopolitanism with two questions we included in our survey. One question asked if news of local affairs is of greater interest than national and international affairs. The other question asked whether greater respect should be felt for people "well-established in their hometowns" or for people "widely known, but who have no local roots." Note that while he characterizes his measure as involving "local community social networks" and also "orientation to community norms and values," his questions are entirely attitudinal and not structural. That is to say, the questions measure cultural orientation, not actual social networks. This observation is made not to be critical of Roof's procedures but to help explain the following apparent anomaly.

We constructed the Local Ties Index, discussed early in this chapter, believing that high scores on it would be reflected in a greater tendency to be interested in local news and hometown celebrities. We thought, in other words, that our index would simply be the structural equivalent of Roof's attitudinal measure. It turns out, however, that Roof's two items from our survey are quite *un*related to our Local Ties Index, taken either singly or together, but they *are* related to our Morality Index. Since, in common with Roof's findings, we too find that local orientation (as measured by his two questions) has some modest impact on religious involvement, it becomes important to determine whether this "localism" factor is over and beyond our measure of moral outlook on religious involvement.

The result is surprising, but in an interesting way confirms and extends Roof's original idea. When the two local–cosmopolitan items are combined and run jointly with the Morality Index against the Parish Involvement Index, the effect of local–cosmopolitanism simply disappears, while the effect of traditional moral outlook remains very robust (the Pearsonian correlation is .41). This result suggests that Roof's items were measuring attitudinal, not structural, characteristics. Our Morality Index is broad enough apparently to have "absorbed" the meaning connected to the two local–cosmopolitan items, depriving them of any independent effect. It is not that a local attitudinal orientation is unimportant in parish involvement; it is rather that the "umbrella" orientation measured by our Morality Index encompasses those localistic attitudes. Meanwhile, the structural dimension of the situation that Roof discussed but did not measure is separately measured by our Local Ties Index.

What, then, is the relationship between local ties and moral orientation? The answer is that they are positively related—i.e., the stronger the local ties, the more tradiitonal is the family/sexual morality—but the relationship is quite weak. The two variables' Pearsonian correlation coefficient in fact is only .069, which means they can be regarded as fundamentally independent. They are, so to speak, two quite different sources of parish involvement.

A Summary

We have two measures now that help us understand differential parish involvement. One is the Morality Index, which, to the degree it reflects conventional moral outlook in the family/sexual sphere, tends to enhance parish involvement. The other is the Index of Local Ties, which, to the degree it reflects embeddedness in a local community, also enhances parish involvement.

What is revealed when the impacts of these factors on parish involvement are analyzed simultaneously? The answer is that high parish involvement rates are seen to vary systematically from fewer than one in ten among those low in local ties and holding the alternative morality to more than seven in ten among those high in local ties and expressing the traditional morality. Chart III–4 conveys this three-variable relationship. The figures on the column tops indicate the percentage highly involved, while the numbers of cases on which the percentages are based are shown on the sides of the columns.

It is easy to see in the graphic presentation of Chart III–4 that, with only slight and insignificant deviations (and allowing for some small base numbers and thus unstable percentages), the rate of parish involvement declines with every step from high to low local ties, and with every step from traditional to alternative morality. It is also clear that of the two "sources" of parish involvement, the Morality Index is somewhat more influential than the Local Ties Index. This latter fact is borne out in a procedure called a "path analysis" showing that the *relative* strength of the Morality Index is .40 in contrast with the Local Ties Index measure of .18. (Some of this difference may stem from the differing quality of the measures.) Together, the two variables account for 20 percent of the entire variation in parish involvement. (Technically, this is reported as $R^2 = .20$.) Surely it is accurate to say of them that they measure two important sources of differential parish involvement.

CHART III–4
Parish involvement declines from 73% to 8% with decreasing traditional morality and decreasing local ties.
(Column height indicates the percentage scoring 4 or 5 on the Parish Involvement Index; number of cases shown on sides of columns.)

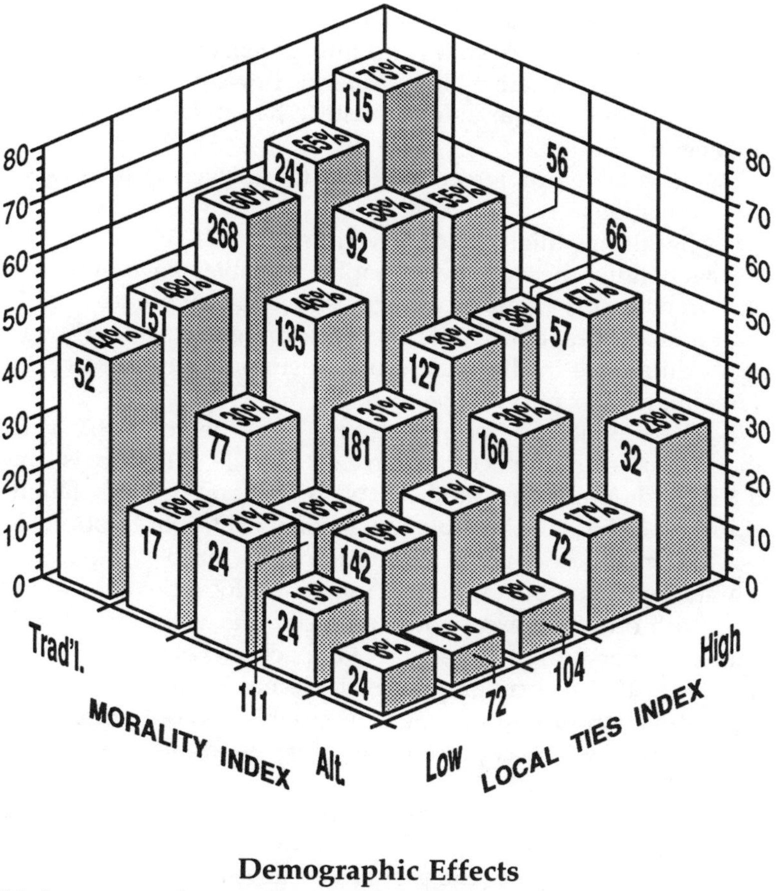

Demographic Effects

We have seen that a measure of local ties plus another measure of morality explain a significant amount of the variation in parish involvement. "Explain" in this context is tentative, however, because many things help bring about people's scores on the indexes of Local Ties and Morality. That is to say, our "explanation" thus far can itself be "explained," thereby revealing more about differential parish involvement and thus ultimately more also about personal autonomy and the process we are calling the third disestablishment.

We have available from the interview nine demographic-style items that are found to influence local ties and/or moral orientation. We want to know, for each of the nine, if a) it influences one or both of these variables and thus parish involvement, and b) in such case, whether this influence flows entirely through one or both of these variables or instead has an independent influence in addition.

The next table provides the figures for answering the first of these questions.

Several things might be observed in Table III–3:

1. Generally, the nine demographic variables have more impact on moral orientation (average percentage difference = 13.2) than on local ties (average percentage difference = 8.9), though again difference in the quality of measurement of the two indexes may enter into this pattern.

2. There is little difference among these demographic variables in *how much* impact they have on average, but there is considerable difference in *which* variable is influenced. Thus, length of residence has considerable impact on local ties but noticeably less on moral orientation. Education has sizable impact on moral orientation but negligible impact on local ties.

3. With only two exceptions (ethnicity and voluntary association membership) the direction of impact—whether positive or negative—that a demographic variable has on local ties is the same direction of impact that that variable has on morality. In other words, whatever produces local ties tends also to produce traditional morality.

How might the set of results be summarized? Generally speaking, the nine demographic variables can be seen as either facilitating or inhibiting the changes we have associated with the post-1960s era. Thus, being a relative newcomer in one's community, Caucasian, single or divorced, male, childless, young, professional or managerial in occupation, better educated,

Table III–3

The Effect of Selected Demographic Variables on Local Ties and Morality

Variable			Difference in %
1. Length of residence in area	10+ Years	Less than 10 Years	
% High in local ties	45	26	19
% Traditional in morality	49	41	8
2. Ethnicity	Caucasian	Minority	
% High in local ties	41	29	12
% Traditional in morality	44	62	–18
3. Marital Status	Married, Widowed	Divorced, Separated, Single	
% High in local ties	42	32	10
% Traditional in morality	50	38	12
4. Voluntary association membership	One +	None	
% High in local ties	45	36	9
% Traditional in morality	40	50	–10
5. Gender	Female	Male	
% High in local ties	43	35	8
% Traditional in morality	48	44	4
6. Family status	Have Children	Have No Children	
% High in local ties	41	33	8
% Traditional in morality	51	34	17

Table III–3 (Continued)
The Effect of Selected Demographic Variables on Local Ties and Morality

Variable			Difference in %
7. Age	43 Years +	Under 43 Years	
% High in local ties	44	37	7
% Traditional in morality	55	42	13
8. Occupation	All Others	Professional, Managerial	
% High in local ties	41	37	4
% Traditional in morality	53	36	17
9. Education	High School or Less	More than High School	
% High in local ties	41	38	3
% Traditional in morality	56	36	20

and belonging to no voluntary association incline persons toward low local ties and toward the alternative morality—and thus toward low parish involvement. To have the opposite attributes, of course, inclines persons toward high local ties and traditional morality—and thus toward high parish involvement.

The question now arises whether these demographic traits, as real as their impact is on local ties and morality, exert impact on parish involvement *independent* of their influence on our two "mediating variables," or are their effects simply on local ties and morality and *thereby* on parish involvement?

To answer this question we use what is called a multiple regression technique, which allows an assessment of the separate effect of each variable on the dependent variable (here, parish involvement) when all the variables in a set of variables are simultaneously entered into the analysis. The result (called a Beta coefficient) thus provides a numerical way to determine a) if there is a separate effect, and b) how strong it is relative to all other variables in the analysis. The following table lists Beta coefficients for all the variables we have so far discussed, presenting them in descending order of their influence on parish involvement. The table also provides the statistical probability that each variable's relationship with parish involvement could have occurred by chance.

It is conventional in social research employing this kind of analytic technique to use a cutoff point of about .10 in determining whether a Beta coefficient is strong enough to attend to. By this criterion, the first four variables in the chart clearly qualify. All the remaining variables are, so to speak, too weak to pay attention to, using this criterion, even though all but "length of residence" are *statistically* significant (using $p. \leq .05$ as the probability criterion).

The question of whether, on the one hand, we are exaggerating the analytic importance of one or another of these variables or, on the other hand, erring by ignoring one or more of them is found in the answer to the following question: How much parish involvement is explained if, instead of looking at the effects of just the two mediating variables of local ties and morality, we

Table III–4

The Relationship of Parish Involvement to Nine DemographicVariables and Two Mediating Variables

Variable	Strength of Relationship (Beta Coefficient)	Probability of Occurring by Chance
1. Traditional morality	.332	.0001
2. Local ties	.158	.0001
3. Gender (being female)	.129	.0001
4. Married or widowed	.111	.0001
5. Member of a minority	.093	.0001
6. No more than high school education	.092	.0001
7. Belong to 1+ voluntary association	.078	.0001
8. Age 43 or younger	−.058	.0019
9. Have children	.053	.0092
10. Professional or managerial occupation	.044	.0249
11. Lived in area 10 years or more	.016	.3851

look at the effects of all eleven variables at once? The two variables alone, it will be recalled, explained one-fifth of the variance ($R^2=.20$). Adding these nine demographic variables increases explained variance by about a third ($R^2=.27$). That is an increase, but it is obvious we have reached the limits of what can be done to explain the overall issue of parish involvement *using the information introduced thus far*. To cite the obvious example, we observed in Table III–3 that length of residence plays a considerable role in the strength of local ties, but when it is put into an analysis that includes the Local Ties Index, length of residence ceases to play an *independent* role in parish involvement. Whatever potency it has is mediated by the Local Ties Index.

Put another way, the two mediating variables discussed in this chapter and the previous chapter are seen here to be very potent mediators indeed. They carry almost all of the causal forces we have thus far encountered.

This state of affairs does not mean that these nine demographic variables are unimportant for parish involvement. Far from it. What it does mean is that such traits as age, education, and occupational status have an enormous impact on parish involvement rates. So do gender, marital and parental status, ethnicity, voluntary association membership, and residential mobility have an impact on parish involvement. *But this impact occurs primarily by changing patterns of local ties and moral outlook.* Thus cultural and structural shifts of sizable proportions—occurring, we are arguing, as a result of the 1960s and 1970s—have had as one consequence a significant decrease in the proportion of Americans who are highly involved in parish life. But have they had the further consequence of changing the cultural meaning of parish involvement? Both of these consequences—of decreased parish involvement and a change in its meaning—must occur if the label "third disestablishment" is to apply. We address this issue in the next chapter.

Chapter Four

Personal Autonomy and the Meaning of Parish Involvement

Until the 1960s the United States had hosted a generally expanding, if peculiarly American, religious "establishment" (see Finke and Stark, *The Churching of America, 1776–1990*, 1992.) Of course, ups and downs can be seen in retrospect, and different denominations held (and still hold) hegemonic positions in different regions of the country. But there were centripetal forces. Especially following the second disestablishment of the 1920s, there was a tendency to perceive a middle-ground religion, a convergence that seemed to include a greater and greater proportion of the American population and led Will Herberg (1955) to declare in the 1950s that being Catholic, Jewish, or some kind of Protestant were but alternative means of expressing commitment to this "established," middle-ground religion and, with it, commitment to American core values.

That "establishment" status was challenged by the postwar cultural and structural changes we have been analyzing. The challenge, we can surmise from our analysis thus far, comes mainly from people who emerged from that period with an alternative moral outlook and reduced local ties—what we in chapter 1 discussed as increased personal autonomy. What, more specifically, might this mean?

Personal Autonomy Close Up
In chapter 1 we offered the term "personal autonomy" as a way of encompassing the variety of sociocultural changes experienced by many Americans since the 1960s and felt indirectly by even more. Many of these changes have no doubt also occurred elsewhere in the world, especially in other industrialized nations where—as in the United States—the hold of a heavy-handed traditionalism had already been broken. But if a kind of rugged individualism which had, so to speak, always been char-

acteristic of Americans now emerged anew in countries long constrained by kinship, territory, and church, the leap in the individualistic direction being taken in America (and perhaps in a few other places as well) took a novel turn. It involved not merely the further weakening of traditional ties but included as well the emergence of a competing legitimating rationale. This competing rationale not only justified further freedoms "from" tradition but also exalted certain freedoms "to" experiment. And the ultimate arbiter of the right choice was to be each person herself/himself. This ideology is what we are calling "personal autonomy" because it has this two-sided nature— not just a readiness to disobey once-legitimate expectations but also a reason to regard contrary expectations as now equally legitimate.

Garry Wills, in a perceptive essay entitled "Mario Cuomo's Trouble with Abortion" (1990), captures the distinction being made here—between disobeying an order otherwise acknowledged to be legitimate and choosing individually to accept a competing order on the grounds of *its* legitimacy. He accomplishes this task by comparing Governor Cuomo's situation on abortion with a similar situation faced by presidential candidate John F. Kennedy.

Cuomo's public pro-choice position on abortion in 1984 had been met by Roman Catholic Bishop Vaughan's declaration that Cuomo might end up in hell. The New York governor took the occasion a few months later at a conference at Notre Dame University to respond. There exist two different claims on Catholic loyalty, he said. One is "well-formulated arguments from a long natural-law tradition" by which the Church addresses "outsiders" as well as members. The other is "doctrinal fiats to its own members [only]." As governor, he could not impose the latter on a public not persuaded by the former.

In 1960 John F. Kennedy, addressing the assembled clergy of Houston, Texas, had invoked this same distinction, claiming that "if the private exertion of authority conflicted with the public appeal to natural reason, he would resign before putting the purely Catholic [arguments] above public arguments from the common good. The clearing house . . . was his conscience."

That argument, says Wills, "was enough for most critics in 1960," and the "religion issue" eventually dissipated. Cuomo's 1984 Notre Dame defense has not dissipated, however, and the Catholic Church, Catholic politicians, and the public at large are very much in turmoil on the *political* issue of abortion. Why, Wills asks, was a position articulated satisfactorily in 1960 found to be inadequate in 1984 and since?

The answer is the "vast change . . . in Catholic attitudes toward authority, especially in sexual matters." Following the Second Vatican Council, which itself did much to allow expression of dissent in the Church, the pope in his 1968 encyclical *Humanae Vitae* continuing the ban on birth control devices "resorted to sheer Church authority where persuasion had failed." What changed from 1960 to 1984 was thus "the attitude toward authority . . . a skepticism that manifests itself in ways going far beyond the issue of contraception itself." (All quotations are from Wills, 1990, 9–10.) Matters of conscience in Kennedy's day were largely rhetorical, it might be assumed, because few persons made claims in the name of conscience alone. By 1984, in contrast, the Supreme Court had granted conscientious objector status even to "nonreligious" persons. Other people were engaging in civil disobedience in the name of conscience to fight for civil rights, against war, for the environment, and so on and on. Persons' internal compasses were now accorded legitimacy, in other words, even when they contravened established ways. Personal autonomy reached new levels of acceptance; various countercultures were not merely "counter" in the sense of deviating from established ways but "counter" also in the sense of offering an alternative rationale for deviating from those established ways.

Local Ties, Moral Orientation, and Personal Autonomy

We saw in the previous chapter a number of factors having an impact on parish involvement—chiefly through the mediating variables we called local ties and moral orientation. Persons high in local ties and traditional in outlook in the family/sexual sphere are, we observed, more involved in parish life. Another way to conceive of this situation is to say that such people have been less influenced by the ethic of personal autonomy, as evidenced by their high local ties and traditional morality. Correlatively, persons more influenced by the ethic of personal autonomy are less involved in parish life. Let us make a more convincing case for this assertion.

As we noted in the last chapter, the Local Ties Index and the Morality Index are only barely related. They are measures that draw upon spheres of people's lives that are hardly associated with each other. How tightly one is linked by friendship to one's community has little to do, it seems, with one's moral outlook on matters of family and sex. And yet these two measures—one structural, the other cultural; one largely involuntary, the other largely voluntary—both reflect the notion of personal autonomy. They differ in the sense that having few local ties, whether from choice or necessity, means more freedom *from* the restraints a community might impose, while holding to an alternative morality means more freedom *to* endorse or practice activities others condemn as immoral. But despite this difference in nuance, and despite their weak statistical interrelationship, both of these measures reflect degrees of personal autonomy—how free an agent a "self" is (or declares itself to be).

Reflect back on the questions making up these measures: How many people in your neighborhood are you really close to? How many of your really close friends live in your local area? Are premarital sexual relations right or wrong? Homosexual relations? Abortion? Gender equality in marriage? In some way, each of those questions touches on the role to be played by individuals' own gyroscopes in determining their own course of action. The questions about local ties indirectly ask about the likelihood of friendship imposition arising from physical propinquity, while the moral orientation questions ask rather directly about the extension of individual rights. Together, as we will now see, these questions reveal a good deal about the social worlds in which our respondents live.

The Personal Autonomy Index is simply the combination of the five-category Local Ties Index and the Morality Index (the latter collapsed at the extremes from nine categories to five).

The result is a 5 × 5 table with everyone assigned a score ranging from 0 (highest in Local Ties and +3 or +4 on the Morality Index) to 8 (lowest in Local Ties and −3 or −4 on the Morality Index). A score of 8 therefore represents the extreme high end of the Personal Autonomy outlook, while a score of 0 represents the extreme low end. As is to be expected, this index is strongly and negatively related to parish involvement. The Pearsonian correlation is −.43, a clearly significant relationship, readily observable in Chart IV–1. Because category 8 has in it only 24 persons, however, in the tables that follow this chart the categories of 7 and 8 are combined.

Of course, the message of Chart IV–1 is a message already received in several ways in chapter 3. Our chief purpose here is to show that the measure we now are calling the Personal Autonomy Index is not just related to parish involvement but related also to a wide range of circumstances in people's lives. Consider first the differing social environments of persons who differ in personal autonomy. Table IV–1 tells this story.

CHART IV–1
Personal autonomy is associated with decreased Parish Involvement

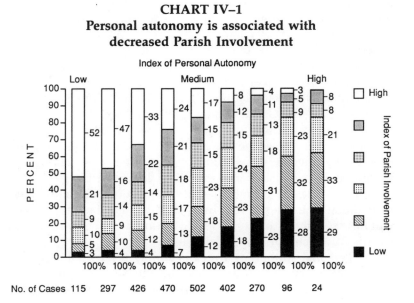

Index of Personal Autonomy

No. of Cases   115   297   426   470   502   402   270   96   24

Table IV-1
Personal Autonomy and the Social Environment

	Personal Autonomy Index							
	Low							High
% *Who Report:*	0	1	2	3	4	5	6	7–8
1. Being very close to many relatives outside the immediate family	70	60	49	39	35	30	29	24
2. Being very close to many co-workers	66	58	47	39	37	35	27	30
3. At least most of their close friends share their ethnic background	74	69	68	63	55	57	51	43
4. Most or all of their closest friends know each other	79	73	53	51	49	43	35	33
5. Feeling an identity with their region	78	68	71	67	64	63	62	53
6. Prefer to remain in their present community	90	82	83	81	80	74	73	58
7. Most of their friends share their religious views	78	71	58	60	54	53	42	36
8. Most of their family members share their religious views	92	88	84	80	73	70	63	51
Maximum No. of Cases*	(115)	(297)	(426)	(470)	(502)	(402)	(270)	(120)

*The base Ns are not the same for all questions since not everyone was asked every question. E.g., the question about close friends among co-workers was asked only of those employed outside the home.

The eight lines of Table IV–1 tell a remarkably consistent story about the social environments of people who differ in their scores on the Personal Autonomy Index. Persons scoring high on the index are far less likely to be close to their wider kin group, their co-workers, or their fellow ethnics (lines 1–3). They also report being in a far "looser" network of friends than do those whose personal autonomy score is low. Thus, not only is personal autonomy associated with lower rates of close relationships in one or another sphere; it is also the case that such friendships as do exist for the personally autonomous are more segmented, as revealed by the lower likelihood that those friends know *each other* (line 4).

Lines 5 and 6 indicate a similar detachment felt more often by the personally autonomous. About three-fourths of those at the low end of the index report feeling an identity with their region (a "New Englander" in the case of Massachusetts, a "Southerner" in the case of North Carolina, etc.), while such feelings are reported by only about half of those at the high end of the index (line 5). Equally dramatic differences are found in answers to the question of preferring to remain in one's current community as opposed to moving elsewhere in the state or to another state or country (line 6). In these findings too, in other words, the more personally autonomous reveal their diminished linkage to people and places.

It is perhaps worth reiterating here what has earlier been said about personal autonomy: it is a two-edged phenomenon. That is, a high degree of it indicates a freedom from or absence of social obligations, which may be isolating and therefore painful. But it also indicates the absence of unwanted commitments or a freedom to ignore certain social obligations, which may be liberating and therefore joyfully embraced.

With that reminder, let us look now at the last two lines of Table IV–1. We see the considerable difference in the likelihood that persons low and high on the Personal Autonomy Index will be surrounded by religiously like-minded people, whether friends (line 7) or family (line 8). In other words, personal autonomy—measured, it will be remembered, by the combination of Local Ties Index and the Morality Index—extends into the sphere of religion by greatly influencing the chances that persons exist in a religiously homogeneous environment. Those scoring high in personal autonomy are considerably less likely to do so.

We can learn still more about the religious environments of persons differing in personal autonomy, however. Table IV–2, identical in format to its predecessor, tells us something more of the religious "biographies" of our respondents.

The first line of Table IV–2 shows us again how nearly universal was frequent churchgoing in the childhood of the these respondents. Perhaps more to the point here is not the high rate of youthful church attendance (which may be exaggerated in recall) but instead the *uniformity* of that rate. It is clear, in other words, that subsequent levels of personal autonomy are not influenced by differing childhood levels of attendance at church. By contrast, line 2 suggests that by young adulthood church attendance and personal autonomy were inversely related, a pattern supported by the results of lines 3 and 4 as well. Line 3 tells us that personal autonomy is strongly related to the probability that people had dropped out of churchgoing for a period of two or more years, while line 4 shows that among those who did drop out, personal autonomy was also related—negatively—to the chances that they returned.

Of course, we cannot infer causal direction here, nor is it necessary to make a causal argument. Common sense would suggest a dialectic process has occurred, with any increase in personal autonomy eroding persons' ties to a church, and any erosion in ties to a church further increasing personal autonomy. What *is* clear from these findings is that personal autonomy is reflected in both the freedom from churchgoing obligations and the freedom to choose whether and how to be religious.

This last claim is supported by the results shown in lines 5–7 of Table IV–2. Line 5 makes obvious the strong negative relationship personal autonomy has with a "conventional" view of the Bible—that it is the "actual word of God and is to be taken literally." The range of agreement with this sentiment—from 75 percent down to 14 percent—is unusually large for a survey like

Table IV-2
Personal Autonomy and Religious Biographies

	Personal Autonomy Index							
	Low							**High**
% Who Report:	0	1	2	3	4	5	6	7–8
1. Weekly church attendance as a child	89	84	85	84	84	86	88	82
2. Weekly church attendance as a young adult	63	50	49	39	35	29	22	21
3. Dropping out of church for two or more years	28	36	45	42	48	55	65	74
4. If dropped out, a subsequent return	69	76	72	60	51	44	37	40
5. Believing the Bible is the actual word of God and is to be taken literally	75	72	65	47	34	27	15	14
6. Believing in reincarnation (that is, we've had previous lives)	17	20	17	26	26	31	34	39
7. Practicing some meditation technique, such as those taught by Transcendental Meditation, Zen, etc.	7	8	8	11	15	15	21	23
Maximum No. of Cases*	(115)	(297)	(426)	(470)	(502)	(402)	(470)	(120)

*The base Ns are not the same for all questions since not everyone was asked every question. E.g., the question about returning to church after dropping out was asked only of those who reported having dropped out.

this one. It must be granted that "half" of the measure of personal autonomy is based on answers given to questions about sexual and family life, and many people find warrant for their moral views on these matters through a literal reading of the Bible. But the other "half" of the index is based on neighborhood and community social ties, not the stuff one automatically associates with religious orthodoxy. The strength of this relationship is thus surprising.

Lines 6 and 7 help us, therefore, by revealing that, unlike orthodoxy, "unorthodox" religion is more likely to be found among the more personally autonomous. The latter are twice as likely to believe in reincarnation (line 6) and three times as likely to practice meditation (line 7). Since 14 percent of the most autonomous assent to a literal interpretation of the Bible, and 17 and 7 percent respectively of the least autonomous believe in reincarnation and meditate, it is clear that "religious orthodoxy" narrowly conceived is not quite what the Index of Personal Autonomy measures. But what it does seem to measure might be considered "lack of conventionality," including lack of religious conventionality—especially the conventionality of the pre-1960s. Put another way, it measures the level of comfort people feel with the kind of religion that was "established" before the 1960s. Those low in personal autonomy may feel at ease with religious pluralism, and they may grant therefore that there are multiple ways to honor and celebrate core values. Such people have adjusted to the "second disestablishment," in other words, but they still feel committed to the existence of core values and believe their own to be among this core—the religious "establishment" of the pre-1960s.

Persons high in personal autonomy, by contrast, have gone beyond the second disestablishment. Religion for them is a matter of choice—both how to be religious and whether to express that religiousness in church. This freedom is reflected best perhaps in lines 7 and 8 of Table IV–1, where we saw that only a third reported that their friends shared their religious views and, surprisingly enough, even one half of their family members appear to hold religious views different from theirs. Obviously a lot of religious heterogeneity is implied.

Personal Autonomy and Denomination

For several reasons, we expect personal autonomy to be related to denomination affiliation. First, there is the known negative relationship (Pearsonian r.= −.43) between score on the Personal Autonomy Index and score on the Parish Involvement Index, and we have already noted (in Chapter 2) that denominations differ in their involvement levels. Second, we saw in Table IV–2 that believing in a literal interpretation of the Bible is strongly (and negatively) related to personal autonomy, and biblical literalism is found to differing degrees in different denominations. Third is the degree to which personal autonomy reflects encounter with modernity—the lack of local ties and the adoption of a countermorality—and this too we expect to find in differing amounts in different denominations.

Indeed, the expected relationship between denomination and the percentage scoring high in personal autonomy is striking. Table IV–3 provides the data, though as in chapter 2 we must, because of numbers, collapse Protestant denominations into "families."

Jews and those without denominational affiliation exhibit the highest rates of personal autonomy. They are followed by Liberal Protestants, Roman Catholics and Moderate Protestants, then Black Protestants, and finally Conservative Protestants. The differences are huge. We can anticipate, therefore, that—because personal autonomy everywhere erodes parish involvement and (as will soon be shown) alters the meaning of "church"—wherever personal autonomy abounds, the effects of the third disestablishment will be more greatly felt. Meanwhile, it is apparent that among those still affiliated religiously, Judaism and Liberal Protestantism appear to be in position to have experienced most the jolt of disestablishment, Conservative Protestantism the least. Catholicism and Moderate Protestantism appear very much in the middle in this regard, as does Black Protestantism. To use the terms employed in chapter 1, the former denominations, if they are important to their adherents, are more likely to be individually important. Conservative Protestantism, by contrast, seems still to be in a position to re-

Table IV–3
Denominational Families and Personal Autonomy

	Percent Scoring High (4–8) on the Personal Autonomy Index	Base N = *
Liberal Protestant	66	181
Moderate Protestant	51	224
Conservative Protestant	29	900
Black Protestant	44	167
Roman Catholic	54	694
Jews	86	49
None	80	342

*These base Ns are not identical with those in Table II–2 because, as will be explained below (chapter 6), a number of Liberal and Moderate Protestants in North Carolina were reclassified as Conservative Protestant, to accord with the particularities of Southern evangelical religion. We have also left out the Other Religious category as too heterogeneous to interpret (N = 39).

main relatively important collectively. But about such refined assessments, more later.

Personal Autonomy and Denominational Switching

Americans change their denominational affiliations with some frequency, especially if they are raised Protestant. Studies estimate that from a quarter to more than half of all adults have switched denominations at least once during their lifetime (see, e.g., Roof and McKinney 1987, 165 and ns. 19, 20). In our sample it is approximately one-quarter, with—as expected—most of the switching occurring between Protestant religious bodies.

Changing denominations can occur for a variety of reasons, of course, marriage between persons from different churches being the commonest perhaps, but so may geographic or social mobility prompt a switch. Even if most switching is "caused" by forces other than theological reflection, however, when it occurs, the *direction* of change is no doubt influenced by religious taste and sensibility. Switching therefore tells us something about how people feel and think about both the churches they have left and the churches they choose to join.

Insofar as switching is a matter of choice, it reflects something of what we are calling an individual-expressive view of the church, and if our argument about personal autonomy is correct, switching ought to be more characteristic of persons high in personal autonomy than of persons low on that measure. It is. While the data are cumbersome to present in tabular form and will therefore not be reproduced here, the following statements summarize what the detailed data show:

1. Using a simple dichotomous measure of personal autonomy (a score of 0–3 on the index vs. a score of 4–8), and using again the classification of denominational "families" presented in chapter 2, we observe that 30 percent of the persons high on the Personal Autonomy Index have switched from the family they were raised in, whereas the comparable figure for those scoring low is 17 percent.

2. The difference in switching rates between those high and low in personal autonomy is evident in nearly all denominational families (the exceptions are Black Protestants, Jews, and Other Religions, where there is practically no switching at all), but is least for those raised Liberal Protestants (3 percent difference) and Roman Catholics (5 percent), and greatest for Conservative Protestants (25 percent). Since personal autonomy is a measure of exposure to modernity, and since of all denominational families Conservative Protestants stand most firmly *against* much that modernity stands *for*, this loss by switching is not surprising. That is to say, Conservative Protestantism staves off loss by remaining firmly antimodern, but it pays a great price by losing its few followers who, in becoming exposed to modernity, accept it.

3. For persons high on the Personal Autonomy Index who do switch, the commonest move is to the category None, outweighing all other moves combined (except for Moderate Protestants, where 19 percent switched to None, and 26 percent allocated themselves to other religious families). By contrast, switchers low on the Personal Autonomy Index most commonly

moved to the Conservative Protestant category, this choice out-weighing all other moves combined (except for those raised Liberal Protestants, of whom 19 percent switched to Conservative Protestant, and 22 percent chose other options).

4. Unusual is the group of persons raised as None. Among those high on the Personal Autonomy Index, three-fourths remain None, while others are now religiously affiliated (e.g., 7 percent are Roman Catholic, 10 percent are Conservative Protestants). Among those low in personal autonomy the contrast is striking; only 40 percent remain None, whereas 50 percent have become Conservative Protestants.

What do these switching patterns tell us about personal autonomy? The main message would seem to be that personal autonomy allows for more individual decision making in the sphere of religion, including the decision to switch out of one's "inherited" denomination, even to switch out altogether. A secondary message, however, is that even though switching to None is the favored path of those high in personal autonomy, nonetheless 38 percent elected to switch into another denominational family.

Personal Autonomy and the Baby-Boom Generation

By restricting our 1988 interviews to persons between the ages of 25 and 60 we had an age spread with 1945/46 at the middle of the range of birth dates. Of course, because of the low birth rates during the Depression and World War II and the high birth rates after the war, we have nearly twice as many in the so-called baby-boom generation (born after 1945) as in the older category (1,690 vs. 924). The question to be addressed now is whether these two generations differ in personal autonomy, as our discussion to now would lead one to expect. The next chart gives the answer.

Two features of Chart IV–2 stand out: 1) Significantly more of the younger generation than the older generation score high on the Personal Autonomy Index; and 2) even so, personal autonomy is not simply a generational phenomenon, as can be seen in the sizable minority of older persons scoring high and the sizable minority of younger persons scoring low. Put another

CHART IV–2

The young (age 25–42) have more personal autonomy than the old (age 43–60)

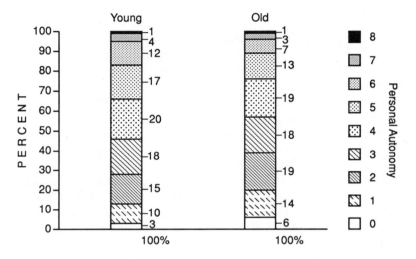

way, the social revolution of the 1960s and '70s—measured here as "personal autonomy"—was real and had real impact, especially on the youth who were coming of age during those decades. But the impact went beyond those people's adolescence; what may have begun on college campuses quickly diffused to many sectors of the population, including working-class youth and older people (see Yankelovich 1974, 1981).

Moreover, personal autonomy has the same kind of corrosive effect on church involvement for both young and old. Among the latter the percentage scoring high (4–5) in parish involvement declines from 73 percent to 16 percent as score on the Personal Autonomy Index increases. The comparable decline among the younger generation is from 60 percent to 11 percent. Once again, in other words, while it is certainly true that the baby-boom generation is less involved in parish life than its elders, it is also true (as we saw at the conclusion of chapter 3) that this difference is largely because of the former's greater personal autonomy (i.e., having lower local ties and holding to the alternative morality). As we have now observed, however, though there are clear differences between old and young—and these differences may be intrinsically interesting—they do not direct us away from the issue of personal autonomy but simply redirect us back to the question of who maintains local ties (or fails to) and who remains committed to the traditional morality in the family/sexual sphere (or adopts the alternative morality).

Personal Autonomy and Changes in Involvement

Without measures from the same respondents at two or more points in time, we cannot know with maximum confidence whether and why changes in involvement come about. It is clear from our theoretical assumptions, however, that we expect changes from low to high personal autonomy to be accompanied by changes from high to low involvement in the church. While we had no way of assessing earlier levels of local ties and moral outlook (and thus earlier levels of personal autonomy), we did ask respondents about their involvement in church or synagogue five years ago. Are they now more involved, less involved, or involved about the same? One-half (49 percent) answered "about the same," while the remaining half reported somewhat more having decreased (29 percent) rather than increased (22 percent) their involvement.

The question can therefore be asked if, as we would expect, those high in personal autonomy are found disproportionately among those reporting reduced involvement, while those low in personal autonomy are found disproportionately among those reporting increased involvement. (No causal direction need be assumed here, since we can expect a dialectic relationship between these two phenomena.) The answer is a resounding Yes to the question. Knowing that people's levels of involvement is influenced by such factors as marital status, parental status, age of children, and health (and thus, for all these reasons, by age), we divided the sample into four age groups (25–33; 34–42; 43–51; 52–60) and then, further, into denominational families. How people high and low in personal autonomy answered this question of increased or decreased involvement could therefore be compared. Jews and Other Religions were too few in number for meaningful inclusion, leaving 5 families × 4 age groups = 20 comparisons. In 16 of the 20 comparisons, those high in personal autonomy responded "less involved than five years ago" more frequently than did those low in personal autonomy. And in 17 of the 20 comparisons, those low in personal autonomy exceeded those high in personal autonomy in answering "more involved than five years ago."

Personal autonomy seems clearly to be linked to level of parish involvement and thus to the process we are calling the third disestablishment. The question now to ask is whether, over and beyond mere level of parish involvement, personal autonomy is also linked to a change in the *meaning* of that involvement. Our theory says that it is—that with personal autonomy comes a shift in the meaning of the church from being collective-expressive to being individual-expressive.

We turn now to this issue.

Personal Autonomy and the Meaning of Parish Involvement

This research, from its very beginning as a speculative presidential address to the Society for the Scientific Study of Religion (Hammond 1988), has aimed to measure the profound change of meaning church involvement has undergone. In chapter 1 we spoke of the shift from religion as a source of primary identity to one of secondary identity. In that same chapter, and several times since, we have spoken of the change in the church's meaning from collective-expressive to individual-expressive. This notion is of critical importance to the documentation of the "third disestablishment" thesis. We have arrived at the point where we know that personal autonomy decreases parish involvement, but now we must ask whether it also—as hypothesized—alters the meaning of that involvement.

Two significant problems loom, however—one a measurement problem, the other a problem of strategy. The measurement problem arises from the sheer difficulty of devising, asking, and getting answers to such a sensitive question as "What do you *really* think of the church?" Obviously that blatant query would never do, but neither could we ask outright whether people go to church more because they felt important others in their lives expected them to go, or more because they had their own reasons and felt that going was a good bargain in their case. More important, we were less interested in eliciting respondents' personal opinion than we were in getting their cultural assessment—what they take as the symbolic character of the church. How this measurement problem was addressed will be discussed presently.

The second problem—that of strategy—arises from the fact that personal autonomy is associated with lower rates of parish involvement, and there is every reason to believe that differential parish involvement *itself* influences the meaning of that involvement. In principle this second problem is avoided by holding constant the level of involvement, thus comparing people who differ (in this case) in personal autonomy but whose involvement level is the same. That is the solution used, but it is used at some sacrifice (such as not being able also to hold constant denominational differences).

The Meaning of Parish Involvement

How did we solve the measurement problem? The interview instrument contained a number of probes that we hoped would provide insight into the subtle distinction we were after— whether the church is perceived to be the agency of social collectivities in which respondents may hold membership and thus express for them their attachments to these collectivities, or whether the church is perceived as a personal agency, to be used to the degree an individual determines its utility. Obviously, neither of these options as stated sounds socially desirable, and just as obviously they do not exhaust the meaning the church might have. Thus, in one question that turned out to be useless for our purposes, respondents were asked, "Do you think of church/synagogue more as a place to worship in community with friends or do you think of it more as a place to be alone with God?" The bait was not taken; 17 percent volunteered "Both," and the way the others answered was unrelated to anything else in the questionnaire. So it was with several other efforts to get people to tell us whether, for them, the church was more collective-expressive or individual-expressive.

In the end, our planned-for ecclesiological subtlety had escaped us in the questionnaire, so we used an indirect method of determining peoples' view of the church. We had several questions that asked in one way or another about the *necessity* of the church/synagogue for being a good Christian/Jew. While it might be argued that regarding the church/synagogue as a necessary means of salvation does not thereby mean it is collective-expressive, the reverse can be argued; regarding the church/synagogue as *un*necessary does imply that individuals can commune with God on their own, and therefore the church is in some sense individual-expressive. Certainly it is voluntarily entered. Out of necessity, we used these indirect items to develop what we call an Index of Church as Individual Choice (CIC). We used four probes:

1. A person can be a good Christian/Jew without attending church/synagogue. (88 percent agree)
2. An individual should arrive at his or her own religious beliefs independent of any church or synagogue. (76 percent agree)
3. One can be a good Christian/Jew and still doubt the existence of God. (43 percent agree)
4. People have God within them, so the church isn't really necessary. (29 percent agree)

These four items are intercorrelated at levels ranging from .21 to .10 (Pearson's r.), and combined they provide an index as follows:

Score	Frequency	Percent
0	100	4
1	390	17
2	802	34
3	692	30
4	359	15

That this index is measuring the sentiment we want to measure is indicated in Table IV–4, which shows how persons with different scores on the Church as Individual Choice Index answered several other questions.

Table IV–4
The Index of Church as Individual Choice (CIC) and Several Other Questions

	CIC Index				
	Low				High
% Who Report:	0	1	2	3	4
1. Church is something freely chosen by each person rather than passed on from generation to generation	57	59	64	68	73
2. One should follow one's conscience even if it goes against what organized religion teaches	57	66	80	87	92
3. Being a church member is an important way to become established in a community	79	71	69	63	46
No. of Cases	(100)	(390)	(802)	(692)	(359)

As can be seen in Table IV–4, the CIC Index correlates as expected with questions having to do with the "inheritability" of the church (line 1), with its authority over individual conscience (line 2), and with its capacity to provide community standing (line 3). In all three instances persons scoring high on this new index are more likely to choose the individualized response rather than the response assigning greater collective meaning to the church.

Parish Involvement and the Church
as Individual Choice

As would be expected, those persons most involved in a parish are *least* likely to score high on the CIC Index, while those least involved are *most* likely to score high. The percentage scoring high (3–4 on the CIC Index) in fact goes from 18 percent of the most involved to 72 percent of those scoring 0 on the Parish Involvement Index. It follows from all that we have learned so far that, if parish involvement is correlated with the CIC Index, so is personal autonomy, though of course the latter is a positive rather than a negative correlation; people with few local ties and who hold the alternative morality—in other words, people high in personal autonomy—are also likely to see the church in individual, not collective, terms. This correlation is what we find (Pearson's r. = +.41).

But the decisive test must now be applied: Over and beyond the impact personal autonomy has on parish involvement, does it also incline persons toward viewing the church as a matter of individual choice? To examine this question properly, we must—for reasons already given—hold constant the level of parish involvement. Chart IV–3 therefore divides respondents first into three groups: the highly involved (4–5 on the Index of Parish Involvement), the moderately involved (2–3), and the least involved (0–1). It then further divides each group into four levels of personal autonomy (index scores of 0–2, 3–4, 5–6, 7–8) and reports the percentage who score high (3–4) on the Church as Individual Choice Index.

Reading up or down the columns makes clear why the level of parish involvement has to be held constant if we are to examine our hypothesis carefully. Obviously, the less involved people are, the more likely they are to view churchgoing as their choice. (Read down the columns.) The critical examination thus consists of reading across the columns, which reveals that, at every level of parish involvement, increasing personal autonomy is systematically and independently related to the increasing likelihood that persons view the church as a matter of individual choice.

CHART IV-3
The view of the church as individual choice increases with increasing personal autonomy.
(Column height indicates the percentage scoring 3 or 4 on the CIC Index; number of cases shown on sides of columns.)

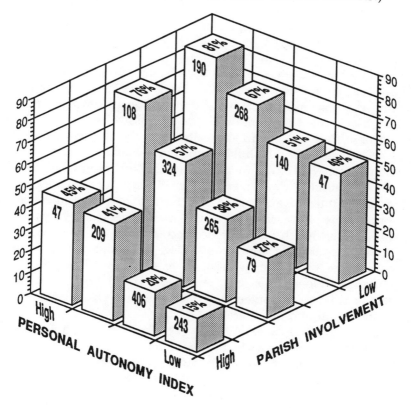

This same story can be told in other terms: Personal autonomy explains 17 percent of the variation in the Church as Individual Choice Index. When the Parish Involvement Index is introduced into the analysis, this amount is increased to 26 percent, but only one-third of the original impact of personal autonomy is mediated through parish involvement. This means that two-thirds of the influence of personal autonomy on people's view of the church is direct and independent of parish involvement.

Further Corroboration

We have yet to examine our disestablishment thesis in the separate regions, that being the task of the next three chapters. For the sample of respondents as a whole, however, the two-part argument appears to find good support; increasing personal autonomy has the effect not just of reducing parish involvement but of altering the meaning of that involvement as well. The cultural symbolism of the church is shifting from a more collective-expressive role to a more individual-expressive role.

Confession was made above that the subtle ways we had hoped to measure this shift had not worked out as planned, and we therefore had to improvise. A check on the improvised measure is possible, however, and the result is further corroboration of this chapter's argument. It is in the logic of the argument regarding the shift from a collective- to an individual-expressive view of the church that churches become more like service stations or department stores and less like social centers or kinship gatherings. Of course, none of these analogies is particularly flattering.[1] Nonetheless, one reasonable expectation is that the shift will be accompanied by a decline in persons' friendships centering around the church.

Once again, to examine this expectation we must hold constant the level of parish involvement, since we can assume the less involved will have fewer church-related friends than the more involved. Our question then is whether, holding involvement constant, people higher in personal autonomy also are lower in church friendships. Our theory would predict so. We use three different measures of parish-related friendships to

---

1. Though there was a time early in the Social Gospel era when the so-called institutional church was held out as an ideal, a church that could serve a multitude of services to a multitude of clients. Riverside Church in New York City is one of many still carrying on such a ministry, and the Crystal Cathedral in Garden Grove, California, is another. Appendix A reproduces their weekly calendars.

Table IV-5

The Influence of Personal Autonomy on Friendship in the Church

		Personal Autonomy Index			
		Low			High
% Who Indicate Church Friendship by:	Parish Involvement:	0–2	3–4	5–6	7–8
Feel closer to fellow denominational	High	59	59	45	31
members	Moderate	30	29	29	28
Feel close to many persons known	High	76	52	33	14
at church	Moderate	35	20	11	7
Most of one's closest friends are fellow	High	43	27	12	12
parish members	Moderate	25	10	8	1

make the test. The first is the question whether respondents feel closer to fellow members of their denomination than to other people. Thirty-six percent of the total sample answered this question "yes." The second question referred to all the people respondents felt "really close to" and then asked about "people you know at your church/synagogue. How many of them do you feel very close to?" Thirty-one percent of the total said "many." The third question again referred to all of one's "really close friends" and then asked "How many of them attend *your* church/synagogue on a regular basis?" Seventeen percent said that "most or nearly all did." Using the same format used in Chart IV–3 (though excluding persons scoring 0 or 1 on the Parish Involvement Index on the grounds that a score of 1 means having only a denominational preference but no membership, and a score of 0 means having neither), we can see that friendships measured in any of these three ways do decline with increased personal autonomy.

Only the second line of the first question reported in Table IV–5, those persons only moderately involved in a parish, fail to provide corroborative evidence regarding the impact of personal autonomy on the likelihood of church-related friendships. But it is the only instance out of the six where support for the major hypothesis is missing. Especially in the case of people high in parish involvement, and especially with the question of feeling close to many fellow churchgoers, we see strong evidence that personal autonomy not only influences the level of parish involvement but alters the meaning of that involvement as well.

Conclusion

We have now concluded the examination of our general argument, advanced for the American public at large—at least insofar as respondents in four states can represent the entire population. Our focus has been on the disestablishment process, as brought on by increased personal autonomy arising from the social revolution of the 1960s and '70s. In the belief that that social revolution has been unequally experienced in various regions of the United States, however, and unequally felt in different denominations as well, we turn in the next three chapters to the analysis of regional and denominational variations on the disestablishment theme. We begin with brief histories of religion in the four states in our sample.

Chapter Five

The Religious Histories
of Four States

Contrasts mark the development of religion in the states of Massachusetts, North Carolina, Ohio, and California. Massachusetts and North Carolina were both royal colonies before statehood, so their early frontier period was one of rough uniformity in religious belief, followed by a period of dissent, and then disestablishment. By contrast, by the time of the Ohio frontier and, much later, the California frontier, this spirit of dissent and disestablishment had become institutionalized, a fact influencing from the very beginning the religious development in these latter states.

This is not to say, however, that Massachusetts and North Carolina followed parallel courses of development, nor that Ohio and California are religiously indistinguishable. Whereas Massachusetts's founding Protestants have declined from a near monopoly in the colonial period to a mere 8.5 percent of the population in 1980 (Quinn 1982, 17), North Carolina's early Protestants steadily increased their membership, so much so that, despite the nineteenth-century legacy of denominational divisions, it remains one of the most stalwart Protestant states (52 percent in 1980) in the union (Quinn 1982, 21). A similar split (in a more attenuated form) can be seen in the two western states. While both Ohio and California developed out of the anarchy of their frontier days and thus became, and have remained, more pluralistic than their eastern counterparts, Ohio has always been more "churched" than California. Thus, 27 percent of Ohio's population claims Protestant affiliation and 22 percent Roman Catholic as compared with California's 15 and 20 percent respectively (Quinn 1982, 22, 11). Within states as well, great differences can be seen, usually between city and countryside. In Massachusetts, for example, immigration and industrialization have concentrated Catholicism in the cities, while most rural areas still reflect the Protestant imprint of colonial times. In the case of California, the north of the state developed much more quickly than the south, but when the south did begin to grow, circumstance conspired to make religion there more powerful than it was in the north. Thus, despite some similarities, religiously at least, each state has its own history and leaves its own legacy. Our purpose here is not to tell these histories in great detail (though a number of citations will lead interested readers to that detail). Rather, we want to provide enough background about the religious development of each state so that the contemporary patterns we will soon be observing will be seen to be not just the products of today's social forces but also reflective of time and tradition. It is central tendencies we are after in this chapter, therefore, not the breadth and depth one might expect of regular histories of these states.

Massachusetts

Colonial Period

During the eighteenth century Congregationalism was the leading denomination not only in Massachusetts but in the American Colonies as a whole. According to Stark and Finke (1988, 43), Congregationalists made up over 20 percent of the churched population of the American colonies on the eve of the Revolutionary War, followed by Presbyterians (18 percent), Baptists and Episcopalians (each with 15 percent), Quakers (10 percent), Methodists (2 percent) and Catholics (2 percent).

Revolutionary War

Immediately preceding and during the Revolutionary War, Congregationalism in Massachusetts was challenged both within its ranks and without. More and more, Congregational clergymen subscribed to liberal, Enlightenment-inspired views concerning the interpretation of Christianity, many becoming known as Unitarians, although their quarrel was not exclusively with the doctrine of the Trinity. Eventually some did leave their congregations to join more "popular" sects, and others formed the Unitarian and Universalist denominations. During the early part of the nineteenth century these new denominations gained support and became a potent force within the new state, although they never became the majority (Fern 1917, 112).

From without, Congregationalists had to contend with the "popular" or dissenting denominations—the Baptists and Methodists especially. The Baptists formed the second largest congregation in the state (Hale 1966, 267), having founded a church in Charlestown as early as 1665. Because of resistance by the established church, however, it was not until the early nineteenth century that their numbers increased appreciably (Platner 1917, 17); by 1811 there were twenty-four Baptist churches in Boston alone (Hale 1966, 267). By the mid-nineteenth century Methodism also began to grow; in 1850 Boston was host to more than a dozen congregations (Hale 1966, 267).

Presbyterians did not grow greatly during the post-Revolutionary period, so, unlike the Methodists and Baptists, they never succeeded in gaining much of a foothold in the state although they retained their colonial status. Their doctrines differed little from the Congregationalists, but their tight-knit synodical form of government was not in step with the independent bent of the established church. Perhaps because they recognized this problem, the Presbyterians formed a Plan of Union with Congregationalists in the late eighteenth century which favored the latter in New England but favored the former elsewhere—e.g., Ohio, as we shall soon see (Platner 1917, 35).

Among the smaller sects the Quakers had some presence, as did Anglicanism (later Episcopalianism) which, because of its obvious ties to England, developed slowly after the Revolution; in 1824 there were four Episcopal churches in Boston; in 1850, eight (Hale 1966, 267).

All told, at the end of the Revolutionary War period there were in Massachusetts 344 Congregational churches, plus 151 churches of other denominations. Among the latter were 93 Baptist, 29 Methodist, and 14 Episcopalian churches. The first Roman Catholic church in New England was built in Boston in 1803 (Platner 1917, 55).

The Nineteenth Century

Despite the challenges, the Congregationalists maintained their numerical superiority in the state throughout the nineteenth century (though a declining proportion of all church members). Unitarians and their cousins the Universalists maintained their membership during the nineteenth century, although their ranks did not grow much during this period. In terms of numerical growth the Baptists were probably the healthiest Protestant denomination during this period, although Methodists also made substantial gains. In terms of financial strength, the Methodists excelled, funding many philanthropic (e.g., Goodwill Industries) and educational enterprises (e.g., Boston University) (Slattery 1966, 458).

Meanwhile, Jews, who had begun arriving in small numbers in Boston and other Atlantic cities throughout the seventeenth and eighteenth centuries, came in large numbers in the nineteenth century. The earlier immigrants were largely from Germany, but later immigrants (1880–1914) came from Eastern Europe—Russia, Poland, Romania, Austria. While Judaism was then, and still is, a minority religion, its concentrated presence in such places as Massachusetts (and, as we shall see, California) has had decided impact on the surrounding religious landscape. In our sample, for example, nearly 4 percent of the Massachusetts respondents identify themselves as Jews. The comparable figure in California is just over 2 percent, and it is below 1 percent in Ohio and North Carolina.

Late Nineteenth Century: Immigration and Catholicism

Despite their growth the Protestant denominations—both colonial and postcolonial—were being challenged. By 1920 the old-stock Yankees comprised only 32 percent of the state's population, the rest being made up mainly of foreign immigrants and their American-born children (Huthmacher 1959, 5). The biggest contingent were the Irish, who began immigrating to the area before the Civil War; by 1920 they and their descendants comprised fully a sixth of the population of the state. But the ethnic character of the immigrant flow had become quite heterogeneous; the Irish were joined by Italians, French-Canadians, Poles and other Eastern Europeans, as well as by Portuguese. The majority of these immigrants settled in urban areas, forming cohesive ethnic communities and thus ethnic churches. Most of these immigrants were Catholic. The transformation of Massachusetts from a Puritan stronghold to a significantly Catholic state is one of the most astonishing changes in the annals of America's religious history. Though subsequently there was proportionate decline, in 1916 fully 71 percent of the state was Catholic (Lord 1966, 533).

Catholicism had been severely restricted in the colony by legislation. Once Irish immigration began in earnest after 1817, however, Catholicism gained a foothold and quickly gained concessions after that; the number of Catholics rose from 100 in 1790 to 3,500 in 1823. By that time Boston counted a cathedral, 3 churches, and 5 priests (Lord 1966, 504–516). With rapid industrialization and the need for labor, the number of Catholic immigrants grew from 3,500 in 1823 to 55,000 in 1846, with 40 churches and 44 priests (Lord 1966, 517–26).

Catholic expansion really began in earnest during the period of the Irish famine (1845–1847), and it was during this period that Catholicism became the majority religion of the state: 200,000 members, 109 churches, and 119 priests by 1866. In 1907 the state had 1.2 million Catholics, 487 Catholic churches, and 1,035 priests; by 1929, the church counted 1.6 million members, 693 churches, and 1,708 priests (Lord 1966, 527–8). Because of parallel growth by the non-Catholics and the staunching of European migration, the 1916 share of 71 percent declined, but Catholicism had obviously mushroomed in Massachusetts after the mid-nineteenth century. In 1980 it still claimed 53 percent of the total population of the state and 82 percent of all religious adherents (Quinn 1982, 17). Protestantism, by contrast, claimed 10 percent of the total population, of which most (85 percent) were members of denominations with colonial roots.

From one standpoint, therefore, the Bay State was transformed from a Protestant region to a Catholic region, although, as with all of the United States, the larger transformation yet was one of pluralization of religion. We turn next to a state where religion, while plural with respect to organization, remains culturally homogeneous even today.

North Carolina

The Colonial Period: Growth of the Dissenting Churches

Although Anglican by royal charter, North Carolina, removed as it was from the older, more established settlements of the New World, generally lacked organized religion during the first few decades. Its broken geography and bad communications hampered the growth of communal settlements necessary for the establishment of a church (Powell 1989, 122). The Church of England did found 22 mission stations in North Carolina between 1708 and 1783 and fought successfully to have its established status recognized by the civil authorities, but it was never very popular. As one scholar put it,

> Non-Anglicans resented its support by public taxes, its control of education, and its other special privileges, particularly the law that permitted only Anglican clergymen to perform the marriage ceremony. The forms and doctrines of the church, the 'Anglican squat,' the church's aristocratic outlook and apparent lack of interest in the common people, its lack of emphasis on preaching, and its lack of emotional appeal met with popular disfavor. (Lefler 1973, 134)

Anglicanism, indelibly linked to British rule, all but disappeared by the Revolution, and the church was officially disestablished during the state constitutional convention in 1776 (Woodard 1983, 216).

Perhaps the most significant development in the religious life during the colonial period was the growth and spread of the dissenting sects after 1730, especially the Quakers, Baptists, Presbyterians, Lutherans, Moravians, German Reformed, and Methodists (Lefler 1973, 136). The Quakers began arriving in the 1670s, and by 1678 the Society of Friends was well organized and continuing to grow, mainly in the central Piedmont region of the colony. Because of their pacifism, however, the Quakers lost both members and the support of their communities during the Revolutionary War (Lefler 1973, 137).

Among the original settlers of North Carolina there were only a few Presbyterians, but with the influx of Scots and Scotch-Irish from Pennsylvania and Scotland itself during the period of

1730 to 1770, presbyteries were established throughout the region on the eve of the Revolutionary War, and they flourished thereafter. Both the Synod of Philadelphia (representing the more conservative form of Presbyterianism) and the Synod of New York (representing the more liberal wing) sent ministers into the region (Lefler 1973, 137–38), thus introducing a subtle split in the denomination which eventuated in the Northern vs. Southern Presbyterian split in 1861 (Woodard, 1983, 225). This split was not formally erased until 1987.

Baptists arrived in the colony as early as 1695, but it was not until 1727 that their first congregation was officially organized. By 1775 there was a total of 16 congregations with several thousand members. It can be noted that even then the Baptists were split into several different groups, so their subsequent fractiousness had early precedent. The first to arrive were the "General" Baptists, who "preached an Armenian doctrine of a salvation free to all, asking no other evidence of repentance, than a desire to be baptized" (Lefler 1973, 138). By 1752 the General Baptists had established 16 congregations totaling several hundred members, mainly confined to the coastal plain.

The most successful Baptist group was the "Separate" Baptists or "New Light" Baptists ("new light" referred to the action of the Holy Spirit which the members of this denomination felt was active among them). Founded by eight families from Boston in the Sandy Creek area of the Piedmont, the church attracted over 600 members within a few years. (Lefler 1973, 140) In 1758 the Sandy Creek Association was organized, and for the next twelve years all Separate Baptist churches in the Carolinas as well as Virginia were affiliated with it.

Next came a more conservative Baptist group, called the Kehuckee Baptist Association (1769) after its location in Halifax County in the eastern portion of the colony. Interestingly, this association united General and Separatist Baptists, not to effect any doctrinal reconciliation between the two, but only because both groups considered themselves too far away from their parent bodies in other parts of the state to govern themselves effectively. Doctrinal differences did however tend to disappear, and soon this association came to include almost all the Baptist

churches in eastern North Carolina. By the time of the Revolution the Kehuckee Association had 61 churches and an estimated 5,000 members (Lefler 1973, 139).

About the same time that the Kehuckee Baptists were estab-
lishing themselves on the coastal plain, a group of "Particular"
(later "Regular") Baptists, distinguished by their semi-
Calvinistic beliefs, were getting established in the Piedmont region. They did not have the same success as the Kehuckee
group, perhaps because of the dourness of their doctrines (Lefler 1973, 139).

"Free Will" Baptists in North Carolina began their history
with the work of Paul Palmer (1692–1763), a General Baptist
preacher whose threefold doctrine consisted of free grace, free
will, and free salvation. By 1800 their total membership was reported at 25,000. Eastern North Carolina was to remain a
stronghold of the denomination (Woodard 1983, 223).

By the outbreak of the Revolutionary War the Baptists were
the most numerous denomination in the state, and the leading
opposition to the idea of any legally established church (Lefler
1973, 140). Not surprisingly, then, it was a Baptist clergyman,
the Rev. Henry Abbot, who proposed that both religious freedom and antiestablishmentarianism be written into the state's
constitution.

German settlers at mid-eighteenth century brought with
them the Reformed and Lutheran faiths, although, because they
couldn't persuade clergymen to reside permanently in their
communities, they were unable to form congregations until
much later in the century. Eventually the Lutherans settled in a
much wider area than did the Reformed and, in the nineteenth
century, became the largest German sect in the state (Lefler
1973, 141). Distrustful of the revivalistic methods of the popular
denominations and aiming at a stricter control over orthodoxy,
the Lutherans established the North Carolina Synod in Salis-
bury in 1803. Most of the Lutheran synods in the South have
derived from this body (Woodard 1983, 226–27).

The Methodists were the last of the large Protestant denominations to establish themselves in North Carolina. Methodist
missionaries, operating as a reform movement within the

Church of England, were active in the colony as early as 1769, but the first official congregation of this church was not formed until 1774. Methodists became a national organization (the Methodist Episcopal Church) in 1784, although a North Carolina Conference had been formed in 1776 (Lefler 1973, 142).

Almost immediately the Methodists experienced several divisions. The first came in 1792 when James O'Kelly and his associates left the General Conference and formed the Republican Methodist church (which later became the Christian Church and is now a part of the United Church of Christ). In 1830 the Methodist Protestant Church became a separate organization, formed from dissidents within the Methodist Episcopal Church. Next, strains created by the approach of the Civil War resulted nationally in the formation of yet another group—the Methodist Episcopal Church, South in 1844—and that split reverberated in North Carolina.

Although Catholics were mentioned as residents of the colony as early as 1737, it was not until 1820 that the first diocese, that of Charleston, South Carolina, was created and a bishop named (Powell 1989, 126). Even a small number of Jews were documented in the colony as early as 1664, but it was not until 1875 that a synagogue was established in Wilmington (Powell 1989, 126–27).

Early Nineteenth Century: The Age of "Methodism"

Albanese characterized the nineteenth century in America as an age of "methodism," meaning that religion came to be regarded more as "felt experience" (Albanese 1981, 99). This religious style—today more often termed "evangelical"—was nowhere more visible than in North Carolina, where methodism in both its nominal and metaphorical senses was the order of the day. In 1775 a revival swept the Carolinas which brought many converts into the ranks of the Methodist Societies; more important was the fact that many people of many denominations were converted because of "felt experience," often at a camp meeting, an open-air style of evangelism which became common for years afterward:

> In the early nineteenth century camp meetings dominated the religious life of many North Carolinians. As the tremendous re-

ligious upheaval known as the Great Revival swept the country from Maine to Georgia, particularly among the Presbyterians, Baptists, and the Methodists, such meetings were used as an attempt to evangelize the whole state. (Powell 1989, 324)

Part of this shift toward evangelical religion reflected the lack of educated leadership, this being a period of profound skepticism among the elite. "Men of education and especially the young men of the country thought it a mark of independence to scoff at the Bible and professors of religion," wrote one Presbyterian minister in 1797 (Lefler 1973, 415). Another reason, no doubt, was the lack of appeal of sophisticated theology to rural, uneducated frontier residents. Whatever the reason, the "methodist" denominations enjoyed phenomenal growth.

On the eve of the Civil War the various Baptist denominations were still the most successful in the state. As one investigator summed up the situation:

With its democratic form of government, simple form of service, emphasis on revivals and emotional religion, and indifference toward an educated ministry, the Baptist Church made rapid strides among the small farmers of the rural districts throughout the state and had more members than any other church in 1860— 65,000 in 780 congregations scattered throughout the state. (Lefler 1973, 416)

Second in size was the Methodist Church which, because of its effective organization inherited from the Anglican Church and modified in America through the use of itinerant preachers, was able to evangelize on a large scale. Moreover, unlike the Baptists, Methodists emphasized both prayer and education, thus enjoying a broader base of support across social classes. So rapid was the spread of Methodism in all parts of the state and among all classes that by 1860 it had more congregations (966) than the Baptists, and nearly as many members (61,000) (Lefler 1973, 417).

Smaller in numbers, the Presbyterians enjoyed only modest periods of growth, though continuing to be the denomination of choice among the urban elite. By 1860 the Presbyterian Church counted 15,053 members (Lefler 1973, 417).

The slowest denomination to grow was the Protestant Episcopal Church, which did not found a diocese in North Carolina until 1817 and was not assigned a bishop until 1823 (Lefler 1973, 415–16). Although it suffered from its second bishop's abrupt conversion to Roman Catholicism, the Episcopal Church did make substantial gains during this period, especially among the educated elite and landed aristocracy. By 1860 the number of clergy had increased to 44, the number of congregations to 53, and the number of members to 3,036 (Lefler 1973, 416).

Among the other religious sects in 1860 the Quakers had 2,000 members; the Moravians, 2,000; and Catholics, 350 (Powell 1989, 326).

Late Nineteenth Century: Reconstruction

The Civil War had an enormous effect on the Protestant denominations in the state. Even before the war the Baptists (1845), Methodists (1844), and later the Presbyterians (1861) and Lutherans (1863) had split north and south over the question of slavery, thus weakening their organizations (Woodard 1983, 222, 231, 225, 227). Only the Episcopalians managed to avoid this regional division. Seizing on this disarray within the traditional denominations of the state, after the war such "foreign" liberal denominations as the Universalists and Unitarians took the opportunity to proselytize in the state, especially among blacks, though with little success. The northern Presbyterian Church also entered the state—to aid black Presbyterians who had left the Confederate Presbyterian organization (Woodard 1983, 227). The northern Methodist Episcopal Church also organized many black congregations in North Carolina. Many black Methodist churches at this time, however, merged with the independent branches of Methodism: the African Methodist Episcopal Church Zion (AME-Zion) as early as 1865; the African Methodist Episcopal Church (AME) by 1868. In 1870 the black members of the Methodist Episcopal Church, South, were organized into the Colored Methodist Episcopal Church (CME), later becoming the Christian Methodist Episcopal Church. Also evangelical in theology and style, these black churches resembled their white counterparts but were organizationally separate.

The end of the nineteenth century, like the beginning of it, was a period of revival in North Carolina, and many of the traditional Protestant denominations began to recover from the Civil War. The census of 1870 documented this growth: Methodists, 1,193 congregations; Baptists, 986; Presbyterians, 204; Episcopalians, 77; Lutherans, 73; Christians, 66. Among smaller denominations but still with more than 10 congregations: German Reformed, Moravians, and Catholics. Quakers began to grow again, fueled mainly by return immigration from the Midwest (Woodard 1983, 218). The smallest groups in the state remained the New England sects: the Congregationalists, the Unitarians, and the Universalists.

Twentieth Century

Despite its growth and its denominational diversity, religion in North Carolina has remained relatively conservative and evangelical (Connor 1929, 695). Thus during the twentieth century the "popular" denominations have kept pace with population growth, and the newer, more radically conservative denominations (e.g., Seventh-Day Adventists, Mormons, Pentecostal and other Holiness groups), though present in the state, have experienced limited growth. Their influence, according to one observer, has been "negligible" (Powell 1989, 696). This seeming irony—that very conservative Protestant groups are less successful where conservative Protestantism is greatly institutionalized—will be encountered again, and discussed, in chapter 7.

In the census of 1916 a total of 50 denominations were listed. Total church membership for the state had increased from 43 percent to 48 percent since 1906. Baptists grew (in seven denominations) from 401,043 in 1906 to over 500,000 in 1916; the Methodists grew from 277,382 to 343,866 during the same period. After these two denominations, we find no change in the order of size from the nineteenth century; Presbyterians were next largest, then Lutherans, Episcopalians, Christians, and Catholics (Connor 1929, 696–97). In fact, this ranking remains pretty much in place to the present day, as we shall soon see, the exception being the relative surge in Catholicism. Though still very much a minority in North Carolina, Catholics now exceed Episcopalians and Lutherans in membership (Quinn 1982, 21).

Ohio

Frontier and Early Statehood (1750–1865)

The facts of Ohio's history are these: while it was colonized in the early part of the eighteenth century, the first permanent settlement was not established until 1750. Cincinnati, the cultural capital of the state, was not founded until 1800, Cleveland a short time later. Statehood was achieved in 1803. Situated behind the wall of the Appalachian Mountains, the territory was settled by a confluence of northern and southern immigrants. Immigration was early and heavy; by 1830 there were more than a million people in the state (Allbeck 1905, 6–7).

In terms of religion the situation was a bit more complex. The social anarchy of early Ohio became a paradigm for the American frontier, endlessly repeated as it advanced westward. For the popular evangelical Protestant denominations, it provided both opportunities and frustrations. On the positive side, for these denominations at least, the amorphous character of the frontier ensured that no once-established church had to be dealt with. On the negative side, the western frontier was even more voluntaristic than the original colonies, and this fact contributed to a very fluid membership in all the popular denominations. Despite such fluidity, however, the lack of stability meant that for some time churches were the chief institutions for social organization, which allowed them to exert a powerful influence in the developing society. According to Miyakaya (1964, 3–9), these denominations were especially important in reinforcing democratic values and the rule of the law. Many churches functioned not only as founts of spiritual wisdom but as courts, both ecclesiastical and civil. Many congregations forbade their members to seek legal redress in civil courts until all the local church options had been exhausted (Miyakawa 1964, 61).

In the early years the two most prominent denominations were the Methodists, from both the North and the South, and the Presbyterians, mainly from the South, specifically the Scotch-Irish from Virginia (Roseboom 1967, 137–38). At first the Presbyterians were the more influential. After the Revolutionary War the Presbyterians had reorganized themselves at the national level, leaving them in a strong position to support frontier church building (Miyakawa 1964, 21). Another factor that aided their cause was the Plan of Union (1801) agreed upon by the General Assembly of the Presbyterian Church and the Congregational Association of Connecticut, which provided that "a congregation of either denomination could select a minister of the other kind of training, the minister retaining his denominational relationship and the church remaining as before" (Rosenboom 1967, 138). Since the Presbyterian Church had a stronger organization than the Congregationalists in Ohio, Congregational ministers tended to associate with the local presbytery, taking their flocks with them and effectively increasing Presbyterian membership at Congregational expense. This is exactly opposite to the situation we saw above in Massachusetts.

As time went on, however, certain factors tended to retard Presbyterian growth. Presbyterian ministers were inclined to form congregations only among existing Presbyterians and neglect proselytizing. Moreover, the Presbyterians tended to be doctrinally rigid and, because of their high educational standards for clergy, often experienced a shortage of trained ministers (Miyakawa 1964, 29). Additionally, revivalism ("felt experience") was and would continue to be a common theme on the frontier, a factor which "tended to scramble denominational loyalties, with especially disastrous results among the Presbyterians" (Allbeck 1905, 12).

Also on the Ohio frontier meanwhile were the ubiquitous Methodists. Although encountering resistance from the Presbyterian majority, the Methodist church nevertheless became a major denomination soon after settlement. Methodism, more loosely structured than Presbyterianism and less intellectual, appealed more to the rural population. Moreover, the use of circuit preachers, welcome sources of news and entertainment as well as religious inspiration, helped to solidify its rural popularity. Many of the region's early political leaders were of this faith (Roseboom 1967, 138–39).

Other denominations were represented in early Ohio: Quakers, Baptists, and after 1830, the Campbellite Christians (Disciples). The Quakers, despite their small numbers, were exceptionally influential because of their incessant social activism, especially in the early abolition movement. The slowest denomination to grow was the Protestant Episcopal Church, which, although present in the region as early as 1792, still maintained only two clergymen as late as 1816. German migration, which began around the turn of the century, brought Lutherans and members of the Reformed tradition, although many of the adherents of these faiths were soon absorbed into the growing Methodist Church. Jews, too, came to Ohio from Germany, founding the Hebrew Union College in Cincinnati as the center of Reform Judaism, a role it still plays.

Catholics were relatively few in Ohio during the frontier era. The first Catholic church was not built until 1818. With the influx of Irish and Germans before the middle of the century, however, growth was rapid; in 1819 Cincinnati counted only 100 Catholics among its residents and no permanent priest, but only seven years later the Catholic population of the city warranted 4 resident priests and a bishop (Roseboom 1967, 139).

Late Nineteenth and Early Twentieth Century: Change and Continuity

Two main themes characterize the modern period in Ohio: immigration and industrialization. Both directly affected the religious composition and tenor of the state.

Unlike the immigration of the early nineteenth century, the later movements brought influxes not only of more Scots, Irish, and Germans, but also Czechs, Hungarians, Italians, Poles, Romanians, Slavs, and Russians (McTighe 1988, 234). As the state grew throughout the nineteenth century, its religious diversity also grew therefore. Although Ohio was a relatively diverse society from the beginning, its diversity multiplied greatly. The 1926 census, for example, revealed that Ohio played host to over a third of the 200 denominations found in the United States as a whole (Pershing 1941, 557), making Ohio the "uniquely average" state in the union. In Cleveland, for example, we see growth not only in the old Protestant traditions but in Catholic, Afro-American, and German Lutheran churches as well as in Jewish synagogues. From 1865 to 1929 the Baptists added 83 churches, the Methodists 26, the Presbyterians 12, the Congregationalists and Episcopalians 18 and 14 respectively. Black religion grew by 50 churches. The Catholic diocese of Cleveland grew by 76 churches during the same period, while the denominations of the German Lutheran tradition grew by 60 churches (McTighe 1988, 233–34). Perhaps part of this growth can be attributed to the fact that both Protestant and Catholic churches encouraged the formation of ethnic churches with services provided in the various national languages (McTighe 1988, 233).

Aside from diversity through immigration, the other great change wrought in Ohio during this period was the increasing industrialization and thus the increasing urbanization of the state. We could use Cleveland as a window into the entire state since, by 1930, 67 percent of Ohio's population dwelt in cities (Pershing 1941, 378). As with Massachusetts, concomitant with the urbanization and industrialization came social complexity and efforts by many churches to adapt to the changes in urban neighborhoods. Some churches even tended toward what was sometimes called "institutionalism"—making the church a community center as well as a worship center (McTighe 1988, 238).

The welter of migrants, coupled with the shift from rural-agricultural to urban-industrial, served to stamp Ohio as religiously "average" in several senses of the term. It did not experience a wholesale shift from Protestant to Catholic, as did Massachusetts. Neither did it remain overwhelmingly Protestant and grow staunchly evangelical, as did North Carolina. Instead it offered "all things to all people" and became "uniquely average." Indeed, in our questionnaire of over 100 questions, Ohioans are in the middle on every single item. It is not surprising that pollsters regard Ohio as the most representative of all the 50 states. At least religiously speaking, that seems to be true. Even, as we will presently see, those denominations we characterize as Moderate stand out in the Ohio ecclesiastic landscape. Perhaps for this reason the modernist/fundamentalist debate of the early years of the twentieth century did not polarize the state as it did, for example, North Carolina (Pershing 1941, 385).

California

The Far West Frontier

Despite the fact that California's European roots via Spain and Mexico were uniformly Catholic, its North American roots were less Protestant than they were nonreligious, or at least religiously fractured. Americans came first to seek gold, and only later, when the mines or the luck of their owners had played out, did these immigrants turn their minds to creating more permanent organizations such as churches. Thus, on the early California frontier denominations were slow to develop. One minister, a "street preacher" named Taylor, heard the rumor on the voyage out in 1849 that there was indeed a church in San Francisco, but for lack of use it has been converted into a jail (Royce 1958, 400). Of course, this was an exaggeration; a Protestant church, a union of denominations, was established as early as November 2, 1848, and by 1849 Baptist, Methodist, Congregational, Unitarian, Presbyterian, and Episcopal churches had been established in San Francisco (Ferrier 1968, 55–60). Meanwhile, the Catholic Church, whose missions had been a major presence in California for over a century, by the time of the Gold Rush was greatly attenuated, there being but a handful of clergy in the state in 1849.

But just as Catholicism was renewed as a result of migration from Ireland, Italy, and France, so did Protestantism respond to the many newcomers. According to Frankiel,

> In 1850, only two years after the great migration began, Protestant churches in California had "sittings," that is, seats in the churches, for twelve thousand people, or 13 percent of the population. San Francisco, though it had the greatest proportion of non-Protestants, boasted twenty-two Protestant churches by 1852. (Frankiel, 1988:5)

By 1853 the state as a whole had approximately 85 Protestant church organizations. "The Methodist Episcopal Church had thirty; the Methodist Church South, twenty; the Baptists, nine; the Congregationalists, eight; the New School Presbyterians, seven; the Old School Presbyterians, four; the Episcopalians, six; the Unitarians, one" (Ferrier 1968, 61). By 1860 many of these churches boasted well-known ministers from the East, many of whom foresaw California as the place where the Protestant experiment would truly bear fruit (Frankiel 1988, 5).

Despite the high hopes, however, the apocryphal story related by Royce is indicative of the general ambivalence toward organized religion that appeared early in California, and characterizes the state to this day. In 1860 only an infinitesimally small proportion of the population actually attended church, despite the huge number of available seats. Indeed, in 1900 only 674,000, or 45 percent of the people, even identified themselves as either Protestant or Catholic (Hogue 1976, 74); by 1940 this rate had fallen to 29 percent (U.S. Bureau of the Census Reports, 1940). As the years wore on, California did mirror the national trend of increasing church membership, but it always remained well below the national average. In our sample, for example, approximately two-thirds of the respondents in the other states claim membership in some religious organization, but in California this claim is made by fewer than half.

Originally, as on the Ohio frontier, churches were welcome agents of civilization, but, according to Frankiel, because of the nature of California's population (young, male, and transient) at the time of founding, only a minority were willing to support churches with more than lip service (1988, 71). The early burst of activity by the major Protestant denominations in California, therefore, stemmed not so much from the enthusiasm of the populace as from the officers of eastern missionary societies who saw challenge and glamor in proselytizing a "new country." Ministers sponsored by both the Home Missionary Societies and the Foreign Missionary Societies were sent to California during this period (Hogue 1976, 65–66).

During the period 1850 to 1860 Protestant churches tried to become a major force in the state, illustrated by their efforts to uphold a sabbath law (Frankiel 1988, 47–58), but California's mobility, pluralism, and all-around tolerance thwarted their efforts. For decades following the Gold Rush, up to half the state's population was foreign born, and not just Spanish-Mexican Catholic but also Jewish, Buddhist, Confucianist, and Russian Orthodox. All, moreover, seemed to be on the move. "So many people of so many kinds from so many places have so rapidly

moved into California so continuously for so long," writes Eldon G. Ernst, "that a distinctive religious environment has
emerged. . . . All conventional notions of a mainstream as over
against marginal religions and esoteric dissent must at least be
qualified" (1986, 48, 50–51).

By the early part of this century, then, the major Protestant
denominations had settled into a secure yet somewhat periph-
eral status. Two things characterized most of these denominations from early in their careers in California. First, given the
state's inherent pluralism, they had to honor each other's identities in order to protect their own, and thus a "gentle and cour-
teous denominationalism, rather than a united front, was the
implicit rule" (Frankiel 1988, 3). Second, the denominations,
perhaps realizing they could never rule from the pulpit, took on
active social roles. They served as watchdogs of government,
for example, and they built schools. Sixty church-sponsored
schools were founded between 1850 and 1874 (Frankiel 1988, 4–
5). They also published newspapers:

> Four religious papers were started in the first three years [after
> 1849]: the *Pacific*, by the Congregationalists and New School Pres-
> byterians . . . ; the *California Christian Advocate*, by the Methodist
> Episcopal Church . . . and later organs of the Methodist Church
> South and the Baptists. (Ferrier 1968, 60)

All told, by the turn of the century most denominations were
represented in Northern California.

Southern California
Denominational developments in Southern California were
different. At the time of the Gold Rush the area south of
Monterey was sparsely populated, mainly with "Californios"
(people with generational roots in Mexico and thus nominally
Catholic). Cattle raising was the major economic base, which fit
well with life on huge, land-grant ranches. Religion was not a
prominent feature of that life, however, because Mexico, having
gained independence from Spain in 1821, showed less interest
in governing Alta California than had Spain. For example, in
1834 the California missions were "secularized" (i.e., the
churches were converted to parishes to be run by secular

priests, not brothers), and most of their land holdings were sold off. The result for the Catholic Church was "dissolution and decline. . . . The vineyards and great spreading ranches of the missions passed into new hands both through Mexican land grants to Californios and subsequent purchase, in many cases by immigrating Americans" (Alexander forthcoming). As North Americans (and foreigners) poured into California after 1849, therefore, they perceived their new home as largely Catholic, but it was Catholicism at a low ebb.

While Protestantism made some effort in the north, south of the Bay Area it was missing altogether. "For sixteen years after the beginnings in and around San Francisco," writes Ferrier, "there was no established Protestant work south of Monterey along the coast, nor south of Visalia in the San Joaquin Valley" (1968, 61). But then things changed. With the coming of the railroad in 1869, over a hundred new communities sprang up in Los Angeles County during the decade of the 1880s. Despite the Catholic traditions in the area, Protestants came to exert a considerable hegemony over society in Southern California in ways they had been unable to do in the north. Considering their feeble beginnings in the north, this development in the south is quite surprising.

As in Northern California, the first ministers who sought to establish their denominations in the southland tried to reproduce their New England model of church polity and, again like their northern counterparts, they failed, though not for the same reasons. Where San Francisco was a boisterous and carefree society recklessly careening toward the future, Los Angeles was happily sleeping in its Hispanic past. The ministers sent west by the home missionary societies were ill equipped to deal with a society which shared none of their Anglo-American assumptions. First the Methodists (1849), then Episcopalians (1851), Baptists (1851), the Methodists again (1853), and Presbyterians (1855) attempted to found congregations in Los Angeles and failed. In 1858 even an attempt to found an ecumenical Protestant fellowship failed, though perhaps more from deluge, drought, and later the Civil War than from lack of interest (Frankiel 1988, 62–64).

Only after the Civil War did Protestantism make headway in the southland, headway which can be accounted for by three successive waves of immigration. First, in the 1850s and 1860s migration from the mining centers to towns on the coast brought Los Angeles its first serious contingent of settled, family-based Anglo-Protestants. Next, after the Civil War, Southern California attracted a number of southern families dispossessed by that conflict and eager to begin again. Such immigration doubled the population of Los Angeles between 1870 and 1880. The third and perhaps most important wave of Protestant immigrants came from the Midwest during the last two decades of the nineteenth century. Many of these newcomers were successful farmers and small businessmen who, having made small fortunes, were looking for a temperate place to spend their retirements. As Frankiel described the situation:

> [This immigration] gradually produced a population in Los Angeles that was significantly weighted toward traditional Anglo-Protestantism. A considerable proportion of immigrants were from midwestern states where the evangelical tradition was strong—Ohio, Illinois, Missouri, Iowa, Pennsylvania, Indiana—while another large segment came from New York. Unlike the gold rush migrants, these newcomers were families and, occasionally, groups of families who came for permanent settlement. Most of them hoped to reestablish in southern California the kind of traditional community that was rapidly vanishing from their home states under pressures of urbanization and industrialization. (1988, 61)

According to Singleton, in *Religion in the City of Angels* (1977), in many ways they were successful. Singleton argues that from 1880 to 1920 Los Angeles was politically under the control of Anglo-Protestants, to the detriment of non-Anglo, non-Protestants of the area (mainly Hispanics and Asians). Additionally, along with their control of political institutions these Anglo-Protestants brought with them the desire to govern education as well, as can be seen in the founding of numerous denominationally affiliated colleges around the turn of the century (Hogue 1976, 73).

Just before and after the Civil War another migration from the South to Southern California began—that of Jews. The Gold

Rush of two decades before had brought some Jews into Northern California, but when Los Angeles was incorporated in 1850, only eight unmarried Jewish men lived there. It was during the next decades that Jewish expansion began, largely by persons moving west from Confederate states. Subsequent waves of immigration eventually made Los Angeles the third largest Jewish community in the world, surpassed only by New York City and Tel Aviv (Hecht forthcoming).

Nor can we ignore the huge number of Mexicans who, during and after the revolution of 1910–20, came pouring into California. The impact on the Catholic Church was of course enormous, though it might be noted that Latin piety with respect to church involvement did not match that of Italian-Americans, let alone that of Irish-Americans.

It was neither Jews nor Catholics that challenged Protestants for the soul of Southern California, however. To some extent the challenge was the same desuetude that had earlier overtaken the church in Northern California. But partly the challenge came from the opposite direction—an enthusiasm for spiritual matters and therefore great competition and challenge from within as well as without the religious community. Southern California has been unusually receptive to experimental religious systems and alien cults. Some are indigenous, but many find their way, drawn by a climate—both physical and social—that is hospitable to unconventional beliefs.

Significantly, therefore, Southern California never became the bastion of domesticated conservative Christianity that North Carolina did, but the reasons were several. First, in the early part of this century California was rocked by the same social unrest, particularly between labor and capital, which other rapidly growing and industrializing states were experiencing. In the face of this conflict the mainline churches of North Carolina stayed on the sidelines, but, according to one observer, the churches of Southern California did not:

> The churches could not, and many would not, absent themselves from these often violent struggles. The Unitarians and other progressive clergy and laity from Methodist, Presbyterian, Baptist and Congregational churches, openly espoused the Social

Gospel; sympathized with labor; worked vigorously to defend Mexican-Americans and Orientals from exploitation. Ethnic churches were fostered by nearly all Protestant groups, and the tensions in the market-place often overflowed into the sanctuary. Clergy were sometimes relieved of their parishes, and congregations split. (Hogue 1976, 74)

A second reason seems paradoxical when California is compared with North Carolina. We have observed already that the latter state, while steadfastly conservative and evangelical in religious style, nonetheless has been relatively inhospitable to this style in its more radical, nondenominational form. Churches splinter over doctrine in North Carolina, but new churches result. California, by contrast, has been more inclined toward religious "movements," which may or may not be denominationally contained. Thus, in 1895 some Methodists in Los Angeles, influenced by the Holiness Movement, broke away to establish the Nazarenes (Hogue 1976, 75). Others, similarly influenced, expressed their Pentecostal enthusiasm in the dramatic Azuza Street revival that went on for several years.

The difference being noted here is subtle, it must be admitted, for surely revivals characterized the South in the last century and may still be observed there. But typically these are church sponsored, not free-floating campaigns as occur in California. Thus, since the 1960s in Southern California a number of movements, having begun on the beach, in a bowling alley, at a drive-in movie lot, etc., have spread nationally. These movements, while often developing into denominational structures, are reluctant to claim affiliation with other churches. They are more often nondenominational.[1]

Similar in some ways are the non-Christian religious movements that have found followers in California, especially in the southern portion. The years of the counterculture certainly

---

1. A recent article in the *Los Angeles Times* reports: "A survey ranking the nation's 100 Protestant churches with the biggest Sunday attendance found that 25 are in California, a state better known for secular pleasures than for old-time religion. The California churches, 20 of which are in Southern California, generally teach a literal Bible, are theologically and socially conservative, focus on the family, have a dynamic pastor and are not aligned with a mainline denomination" (John Dart, *Los Angeles Times*, 12 Oct. 1990).

made such movements more visible (and created yet others), but it should be recognized that Eastern-oriented theologies and philosophies in California go back well before the 1960s, as do the religion-like movements that honor nature, seek health, or cure the mind. Oddly, then, Southern California in the twentieth century may have more in common with the frontier period of North Carolina than it does with the contemporary South.

All of this leaves so-called mainstream religion in Southern California in pretty much the same position we saw in Northern California—not out of the picture entirely, but certainly on the periphery, visible and newsworthy but not central to other social institutions. It will come as no surprise to see, in the next chapter, that California has by far the lowest rate of church membership but also the highest rate of people who meditate and believe in reincarnation. But that has probably been true since the Gold Rush.

Summary

We will pick up the more recent story of religion in these four states in the next chapter. Our purpose here has been to give enough historical context to allow each state's unique profile to be seen, since the four states were selected in this investigation to represent distinctive regions. A brief summary of each profile is thus in order.

1. Massachusetts: Founded by persons whose religious organizations were to become America's liberal Protestant denominations, Massachusetts Protestantism has remained significantly liberal in its religion. In the nineteenth century the liberal denominations began sharing the Protestant population with so-called moderate denominations, especially Baptist and Methodist, but the larger transformation came from the immigration of Roman Catholicism, which became the majority religion in the state, plus a small but strategic presence of Judaism.

2. North Carolina: Although originally Anglican (Episcopalian), this state rather quickly adopted a revivalistic, emotional style of religion associated with the Baptist and Methodist denominations. Most church-affiliated North Carolinians, black

and white, have been and still are members of one or the other of these traditions. Their conservative evangelicalism is not shared by the small minority who are Congregational (United Church of Christ), Episcopal, Lutheran, Quaker, etc., or another minority who are Catholic. Nonetheless, this "southern religion" comes as close to being an "established" religion as can be found in any of these four states.

3. Ohio: Settled during the time that the Baptists, Methodists, and Disciples were dominating religion on the frontier, Ohio became strongly moderate in denominational outlook. The influx of immigrant Lutherans added to this moderate climate, as did the moderate amount of Catholics of various ethnic backgrounds. Ohio is an "average" state from many perspectives, including the religious.

4.California: With a Catholic mission heritage that nearly disappeared, Californians who developed this territory into an American state were relatively unconcerned about religion. Of course, virtually all denominations known elsewhere found some followers here, as did a few religious movements found nowhere else. Californians, it might be said, are more "spiritual" than they are "ecclesiastic."

We have carried this storytelling into the twentieth century, but the religious developments in these four states since World War II, and especially since the 1960s and '70s, have yet to be described. We pick up the story line in the next chapter.

Chapter Six

From Regional Histories
to Religious Climates

We have been operating on the assumption that, while in a technical sense no state in the United States has had an established church since Massachusetts was the last to disestablish in 1833, most states throughout the nineteenth century were heavily "Protestantized." If not the *established* religion, Protestantism was at least the *establishment's* religion in most regions of the country. As Albanese puts it:

> Different movements and traditions seemed to take on some of the characteristics of the Protestant mainstream. . . . There were numerous ways that the boundaries of the separate traditions were overlapping the boundaries of Protestantism. . . . By saying that Protestantism acted as the dominant and public religion of the United States, we are saying that Protestantism became the one religion of the country. Whatever it meant in the personal lives of millions of individuals, publicly Protestantism meant acknowledged ways of thinking and acting supported by most institutions in society—by the government (though unofficially), the schools, the media, and countless Protestant churches and families. (1981, 248)

This Protestant hegemony had pretty much evaporated by the 1920s, however, at least in urban areas outside the South. Not only did religious liberty assure non-Protestants eventual parity, but also the relationship between religion of any sort and the other institutions of society underwent a transformation. Though not occurring all at once or everywhere at the same time, religious choices were becoming less distinctive, religious boundaries less clear. Optimists could see this change as a celebration of unity in diversity, while pessimists noted that religion was becoming a lukewarm pastime. Those who dissented from this viewpoint were, at mid-century, either in self-isolation, like the Amish or Hasidic Jews, or otherwise largely invisible to the wider society, like Fundamentalists or

Theosophists. The consequence was a fairly pervasive "republican religion," thoroughly pluralistic yet at ease with America's
procedures, if not all its practices.

It was this fairly pervasive, reasonably complacent religion—
a religion at home with its host culture—that got shaken in the
1960s and '70s, to a point where the idea of a third disestablishment seems appropriate. A presumptive Protestantism had
given way earlier in the century to a presumptively American
religion, but now the notion of "presumptive" religion itself was
being challenged.

Obviously, however, what was being challenged differed
from one region of the country to another. We have already
sketched the religious histories of our four states, bringing their
stories into the twentieth century. Let us pick up the story at the
point where the "republican religion" was at its zenith.

Religious America in the 1950s

After a loss of vitality brought on by the Great Depression and
World War II, churches in the United States experienced a remarkable period of growth—in members, attendance, church
building, and financial support. Some of this growth can be attributed to the unleashing of forces that had been inhibited for
one and a half decades (e.g., lack of money and leaders), but a
significant amount of growth came about because, beginning in
1946, Americans began producing children in record numbers.
While this record "baby boom" went on for twenty years, the
first wave of children began reaching Sunday school age in the
1950s, a phenomenon that brought them and their parents into
the orbit of churches. Combined with the frantic creation of new
towns and suburbs, which meant also the location of new
churches, this flooding of churches by young families led to
new highs in parish involvement. It is not surprising, therefore,
that only 5 percent of our respondents report never attending
church (or attending only on holidays) when they were age 8 to
10, and fully 85 percent report having attended weekly. Church
business was booming.

What was the picture in each of our four states? We have seen
how much the states differ in denominational profile, so we

must, in looking at a state, take into account its unique history. One way of doing so is to group denominations into families, as we did in chapters 2 and 4. Because there are not enough Episcopalians in any one state, we group that denomination together with other "Liberal" Protestants. Other denominations are grouped as "Moderate" Protestants, yet others as "Conservative." Roman Catholics are treated as a single group for our purposes here, even though ethnic differences are known to exist (and our four states differ in the incidence of ethnic parishes). Jews, too, though divisible into Reform, Conservative, and Orthodox, must be treated as one group because of limited numbers.

Denominational Families in Four States, 1952

We changed the basis of the grouping procedure from chapter 2 to chapter 4 in the case of Protestants in North Carolina, and now is the time to describe what we did. Samuel S. Hill, a leading historian of southern religion, asserts that Methodists, Presbyterians, and Disciples in the South resemble Southern Baptists more than they do their northern denominational counterparts. He writes:

> It would be difficult to disprove the oft-heard dictum that greater similarity obtains among Baptist, Methodist, and Presbyterian churches in the South than between an average southern regional church in any one of these denominations and its northern counterpart. . . . Outsiders are often unprepared for the high degree of similarity between . . . them and other such major families as . . . Disciples of Christ, the Church of Christ, the Assemblies of God, and the Church of the Nazarene. (1966, 20–22)

We have accordingly moved Presbyterians in North Carolina from the Liberal category, and moved Methodists and Disciples from the Moderate category, relocating all three in the Conservative Protestant category. The consequence, of course, is greatly attenuated numbers of Liberal and Moderate Protestants in North Carolina, but the basis for this decision seems firm. Every time two or more entities are combined, whatever distinguishes them from each other is lost, but if what they share is more important than how they differ, combining is justified. The history of conservative evangelicalism's growth and dominance in North Carolina is the justification in this case.

With this caveat, then, let us look at the distribution of denominational families in four states. The legacies traced in the previous chapter are very visible.

Appendix D of Edwin S. Gaustad's *Historical Atlas of Religion in America* (1976 ed.) provides, for all Christian churches in 1952 having at least 100,000 members nationwide, their number of churches in each state. Because smaller religious bodies are not included, these figures underestimate the absolute number of churches. And because denominations differ in how big or small an ideal parish is thought to be, no inference regarding membership size from numbers of churches is possible. Despite these limitations, however, the figures of Table VI–1 show an interesting (and enduring) pattern.

The dominance of Conservative Protestantism in North Carolina is the most pronounced figure in this entire table. Even if Methodist, Presbyterian, and Disciples churches were removed from the category Conservative Protestant, it would remain the largest in the table, at 51 percent. Only Moderate Protestant

Table VI–1
Proportion of Churches in Four States That Are Liberal, Moderate, or Conservative Protestant, or Catholic, 1952

	NC	OH	MA	CA
Liberal Protestant	7.2%	14.5%	35.8%	16.3%
Moderate Protestant	2.6	48.2	28.2	27.3
Conservative Protestant	88.5	25.8	6.1	42.6
Roman Catholic	1.7	11.5	29.9	13.8
	100%	100%	100%	100%
No. of churches	7,728	7,562	2,388	5,569
Population in 1950 (in 000s)	4,062	7,947	4,691	10,586
No. of inhabitants per church	562	1,051	1,964	1,901

churches in Ohio and Conservative Protestant churches in California approach majority status in their states, but the conservative evangelical type of church clearly sets the tone in North Carolina as no other type of church does in the other states. Roman Catholic parishes in 1952, for example, were pretty scarce in the Tarheel state (131 churches).

Ohio, by contrast, had 870 Catholic churches, or nearly 12 percent of the churches of the larger Christian denominations in that state. Liberal Protestants are somewhat better represented, and certainly Conservative Protestants are, perhaps reflecting not only the early migration into frontier Ohio from the South but also the borders it shares with Kentucky and West Virginia. Most striking, however, is the degree to which Moderate Protestant churches predominate in Ohio. The comparison with North Carolina is meaningless because of the arbitrary subtraction of Methodists and Disciples we undertook there, but the comparisons with Massachusetts and California are significant. The midwest success of the post–Revolutionary War and immigrant Protestant churches was still starkly evident in Ohio in 1952, in contrast to their lesser impact on either coast.

Massachusetts had still a plurality of Liberal Protestant churches, though Catholic parishes were a strong second in 1952. Conservative Protestant churches, while not as scarce as Roman Catholic churches in North Carolina, were still pretty rare in the Bay State.

In vivid contrast, in California attention must be paid to the predominance of Conservative Protestant churches, equal in number to the Liberal and Moderate categories combined. By 1952, California had experienced two sizable recent migrations from the South—those coming during the 1930s Depression and those who were drawn to the West Coast wartime industry. Roman Catholicism, with about 14 percent of the churches in 1952, maintained a significant presence, understated here (and in all states) because Catholic parishes tend on average to serve many more members than do churches of other denominations. (By this same reasoning, Conservative Protestant churches, which tend to be small, are overstated here.)

What we see in 1952, then, is remarkably reflective of the histories briefly reviewed in the previous chapter. North Carolina remained an evangelical region; Ohio was still dominated by Moderate Protestantism and remained "uniquely average"; Massachusetts in 1952 retained a Liberal Protestant cast, though this leadership was by now shared by Catholics and Moderate Protestants. California's fluidity appears to have continued its role on the religious scene, giving Conservative Protestantism there a share of churches exceeded only in North Carolina.

Regarding California and North Carolina, however, there is reason to believe that the category Conservative Protestant already had, by 1952, quite different meanings in the two states. Fully 86 percent of these churches in North Carolina (using the narrower definition of Conservative Protestant, the one used outside of North Carolina) were Southern Baptist. By contrast, in California, only 19 percent were Southern Baptist, the other 81 percent being churches of Conservative denominations more prevalent on the West Coast than in the South—e.g., Seventh-Day Adventist (316 parishes in California; 57 parishes in North Carolina), Assemblies of God (597:48), Church of the Brethren (32:24), Church of God, Andersonville, Indiana (96:41), Church of God in Christ (229:55), Church of the Nazarene (239:40), Missouri Synod Lutheran (241:29), Free Methodist (64:3). Indeed, of all the Conservative denominations reported by Gaustad, only the Church of God, Cleveland, Tennessee (64:223), joins the Southern Baptist in being better represented in North Carolina than in California. One might hazard the guess that even in 1952 to be a Conservative Protestant in North Carolina was to blend into the sociocultural landscape, whereas in California it was an expression of dissent. We will return later to this idea.

Before leaving Table VI–1, however, a comment is required about the table's bottom line, the ratio of people to churches. Roughly speaking, North Carolina has nearly twice the number of churches per population that Ohio has, and nearly four times the number that Massachusetts and California have. By noting further that Massachusetts is far more Catholic (whose parishes tend to be large) while California is far more Conservative Protestant (whose parishes tend to be small), we can infer that, despite similar parish-to-people ratios, Massachusetts has far more church-related persons than California. The latter remains ecclesiastically lukewarm, relatively speaking.

We turn now to adherents rather than churches, and we come forward in time.

Denominational Families in Four States, 1971–1980

For 1971 and again in 1980 Quinn and his associates assembled church "adherent" data for every county in every state of the United States for all denominations that would cooperate.[1] Some, such as Christian Scientists and Orthodox Jews, did not on principle cooperate, and other religious bodies for other reasons no doubt slipped through the cracks and were not counted. These groups are numerically small, however, which means that a territory as large as a state will have its denominational portrait altered very little as a result of this loss.

Another concern, of importance for some purposes but not terribly important to the concern here, is the precision with which cooperating bodies reported their data. Errors of course crept in. But the most likely outcome of such accumulated errors is a kind of "canceling out." We have no reason, for example, to assume that one state was more careless than another, that one denomination was more careless than another, or that more carelessness occurred in 1971 than in 1980. One would be ill advised to take any one church's report at face value, but the larger picture, and changes in that picture from one decade to the next, are reasonably trustworthy. Moreover, they are the best data available.

Table VI–2 therefore provides, for each state at two time periods, the percentage of the population who have a Christian denominational adherence (preference) and—for those who do have a preference—the proportion who are Liberal, Moderate,

---

1. They also provide church membership data, but because denominations differ in requirements for membership, we use the "adherent" figure. This is more or less an approximation of our questionnaire's "denominational preference," except it is supplied by religious organizations, not individuals. Thus, more of the public at large will, when asked, be able to name an affiliation than the organizations they name will be aware of them.

or Conservative Protestant, or Roman Catholic. In North Carolina we again classify Presbyterians, Methodists, and Disciples as Conservative on the grounds that they resemble the dominant Southern Baptists more than their nonsouthern counterparts.

What do we learn from Table VI–2? A first bit of knowledge is contained in the top row in each half of the table: The percentage of affiliated Christians actually increased during the decade of the 1970s. Surely this fact is contrary to the perception of eroding church affiliation, though of course it says nothing of the level of that continued affiliation. (We explore that question

Table VI–2

Proportion of Adherents in Four States Who Are Liberal, Moderate, or Conservative Protestants, or Catholic, 1971, 1980

1971	NC	OH	MA	CA
% of the State's Population Adhering	50.6%	47.0%	63.0%	33.1%
Liberal Protestant	5.1	13.4	11.0	8.8
Moderate Protestant	4.2	28.7	5.4	13.0
Conservative Protestant	87.9	12.8	1.6	18.7
Roman Catholic	2.8	45.1	82.0	59.5
	100%	100%	100%	100%
1980				
% of the State's Population Adhering	53.9%	48.7%	63.3%	33.8%
Liberal Protestant	4.5	11.5	9.3	7.1
Moderate Protestant	3.7	25.1	5.2	10.1
Conservative Protestant	88.9	17.2	1.8	23.3
Roman Catholic	2.9	46.2	83.7	59.5
	100%	100%	100%	100%

soon.) More surprising yet is to find that Massachusetts has the highest proportion of church-affiliated persons. Its rate in both decades is nearly two-thirds, compared with Ohio's and North Carolina's one-half and California's one-third. Almost certainly this high rate in Massachusetts is accounted for by the large number of Catholic parishes that count as adherents many persons who are "in" a parish but not "of" it.

Table VI–2 also tells us that the picture drawn from the number of churches in 1952 (Table VI–1), which accorded so well with the history of each state, is a picture that continues as an accurate portrayal into the late twentieth century. That is, Conservative Protestantism dominates the North Carolina religious scene, Moderate Protestantism has its greatest strength in Ohio, Liberal Protestants outnumber other Protestants in Massachusetts but are themselves far outnumbered by Catholics, and California has relatively few adherents (though six out of ten adherents are Catholic, and Conservative Protestants exceed Liberal and Moderate Protestants combined).

If Table VI–2 is seen in "market-share" terms, one can ask about gains and losses of denominational families' share of religion consumers. From this perspective Catholicism has experienced little change at all. Liberal Protestants have lost heavily in all four states, as have Moderate Protestants everywhere but Massachusetts. The big gainers are the Conservative Protestants, especially in Ohio and California. North Carolina is an exception, in part perhaps because it had already saturated its market by 1971.

The Situation in 1988

Tables VI–1 and VI–2 have the limitation of reporting data supplied by churches, and churches are known to have faulty records when it comes to who is a member or who is an adherent. As we said before, for interstate comparisons these inaccuracies may not matter much because to the degree they occur everywhere, the *relative* data will be reasonably correct.

In the interview setting these inaccuracies can be eliminated, though there is the potential problem of respondents' truthfulness and—more serious—whether interviewer and interviewee mean the same thing by such terms as "member," "preference," "attendance," etc.

All of this discussion is simply to prepare readers for the next table, showing in each state how the respondents in the telephone survey answered the question about their current denominational preference. (We continue with the augmented category of Conservative Protestant in North Carolina.) This method allows us also to report Black Protestants, Jews, and persons preferring some "Other" religion. Instead of counting Christian adherents and subtracting from the total population to learn the proportion "unchurched," we have instead persons' responses telling us that they have *no* religious preference, a more reliable indication of nonaffiliation (and the basis on which such persons were scored 0 on the Parish Involvement Index).

There is another factor keeping the next table from being directly comparable to Table VI–2. Just as church record keeping can contain errors, so can the telephone survey have biases. For one thing, respondents by definition have a telephone, and therefore we doubtless missed the very poor, the homeless, the hospitalized, etc. Second, we limited our sample to people between the ages of 25 and 60, which of course church records do not. Finally, there is always the question of "representativeness"—whether the persons who cooperated in the interview are "just like" those who refused to respond. One would assume not, but how much the refusers differ, and along what lines, is unknown. While these biases mean that our statistics cannot be exact, we can use them to compare states and assess change through time.

Table VI–3 provides the data.

A number of features of Table VI–3 are worth noting, some indicative of change since 1971 and 1980 and others reflecting long-term continuity. Remembering that direct numerical comparisons are improper for reasons given above, we can nonetheless observe the following:

1. Many more people claim a religious preference than Christian churches claim as adherents. Either there are far more non-Christians than supposed, or there are far more persons

Table VI–3

Religious Preferences in Four States, 1988

	NC	OH	MA	CA
(% Claiming a Preference)	94.0	90.9	82.4	80.9
Liberal Protestant	3.3	6.2	13.3	10.0
Moderate Protestant	1.8	20.1	5.4	12.5
Conservative Protestant	74.2	34.0	15.2	32.4
Black Protestant	13.1	6.8	1.9	7.2
Roman Catholic	6.2	30.6	57.9	31.7
Jewish	.7	1.1	4.4	2.8
Other Religion	.7	1.2	1.9	3.4
	100%	100%	100%	100%

preferring small denominations that did not get counted, or—what is probably the case—in a telephone interview almost everybody can state a "preference" if asked, even if it has been years since they darkened a church door. Thus, while the range of "preference" is 81 percent in California to 94 percent in North Carolina, the range of actual membership in a church or synagogue, as claimed by our respondents, is 49 percent in California to 72 percent in North Carolina.

2. In North Carolina, with the exception of some increase of Catholics, the 1988 picture resembles that of 1980 and 1971 (and even the distribution of churches in 1952). Without Methodists, Presbyterians, and Disciples, the Liberal and Moderate Protestant categories are little more than token denominations in North Carolina, Jews and Other Religions even more so.

3. In Ohio, Moderate Protestants still retain their greatest representation relative to the other states, but they have been overtaken by Conservative Protestants, who have even surpassed Catholics in this set of data. (This second change also occurs in California, where Conservative Protestants were outnumbered by Catholics by three to one in 1971, but now show a slight edge.)

4. Massachusetts shows a different kind of change. It has a significant minority of Jews, and Other Religions can claim some representation, but Catholics are still in the majority. However, their proportion has declined significantly. Two things no doubt account for this decline in market share: One is the much greater growth of Conservative Protestantism from 1971 and 1980 to 1988. The other is the phenomenal change in nonadherents in Massachusetts. This second change is not easy to see in comparing Table VI–2 with Table VI–3 because of the difference in the tables' contents, but note that in the earlier period Massachusetts church record keeping would suggest that it had by far the highest rate of adherence among the four states. By 1988, and by the testimony of persons themselves, Massachusetts's nonadherence had dropped nearly to the rate in California, a state long recognized as very "unchurched." Both of these categories—Conservative Protestantism and the "unchurched"—must have recruited Catholics in large numbers. We will see in the next chapter that they indeed have.

Liberal and Moderate Protestants in Massachusetts might be thought to be retaining their relative positions (e.g., Liberals maintain a two-to-one lead over Moderates, and Liberal Protestants enjoy a larger market share here than in any of the other three states), but note that in the 1988 self-designating preference scheme, Conservative Protestants are nearly the equal of Liberal and Moderate Protestants combined. It might be accurate to describe Massachusetts as the state among these four experiencing the greatest religious changeover in recent decades.

5. Finally, California. Its picture resembles that of Massachusetts, though its changes appear on a less dramatic scale. Catholics here have been historically strong, and they remain so, even though they are losing market share chiefly to Conservative Protestantism and especially to the nonaffiliated. Conservative Protestants have continued to increase, but they had already surpassed other Protestants by 1971.

Black Protestantism has a significant minority in California (just as it does in Ohio, though neither state compares with North Carolina in this regard), as does Judaism. Perhaps not surprising is the relatively strong presence of "other religions," not only more prevalent in California than in the other states but actually more prevalent than Liberal and Moderate Protestants in North Carolina, and more prevalent than Jews in all but Massachusetts. The fact that "other religions" are rarest in North Carolina only underscores that state's religious traditionalism, even as it reflects California's openness to religious innovation (Wuthnow, 1976, 1978).

We have, then, evidence both for change and for continuity. Change has clearly been least in North Carolina, continuity most. Ohio is next in this regard, while Massachusetts and California together exhibit the most change. These latter two states differ from one another, however, in the sense that Massachusetts's changeover is fairly recent, whereas California has experienced so much change for so long that any continuity at all is hard to find. We can explore this kind of comparison by utilizing yet other questions from the interviews.

Regional Religious Climates

We begin by exploring regional variation in what we will call religious "climates," a term usefully vague in that it suggests a contextual condition, potentially important to everyone existing within it, whether or not everyone contributes to it. Thus if "nearly everyone" goes to church in a certain locale, then even those who do not go may be influenced by the "nearly everyone goes" climate. The religious climates of our four states are remarkably different, as we will now see.

Organizational Involvement in the Church

No doubt the easiest kind of regional religious difference to understand is people's formal association with religious organizations—churches. Table VI–4 provides three pieces of information bearing directly on state-by-state comparisons of this kind.

Most important in this table is the information in line 1—the current levels of parish involvement—whether measured by the median score on the Parish Involvement Index, by the percentage scoring 4–5, or by the percentage scoring 0 on that index. The four states differ considerably. Between North Carolina and Massachusetts there is more than a full-step

Table VI–4

Organizational Involvement in the Church in Four States

	NC	OH	MA	CA
1. Parish Involvement				
Median Index Score	2.99	2.55	1.88	1.57
% Scoring 4–5	50	43	32	30
% Scoring 0	6	9	16	15
2. % who ceased church attendance for 2+ years	35	44	51	59
3. Of those who dropped out for 2+ years, the % who returned	67	57	49	49
No. of cases*	(649)	(661)	(655)	(655)

*Base Ns vary since not everyone answered every question.

difference in median involvement levels, while between North Carolina and California this difference approaches one-and-a-half steps. Ohio, though with a significantly lower rate than North Carolina, nonetheless resembles the state to its south more than the states on either coast. A similar story is told in the row of percentages scoring 4 or 5 on the index.

This pattern, in mirror image, is then duplicated with the percentage scoring 0 on the Parish Involvement Index. North Carolina is lowest, Ohio next, and the other two states are considerably higher. Since this score, by definition, was given to persons who responded that they have no current religious preference, this row of figures, like the row above it showing rates of high involvement, confirms what the comparative median scores have indicated.

Indirect confirmation of this pattern is found in line 2, where dropout rates are compared. Once again North Carolina is at one extreme, California at the other, with Ohio closer in rate to the former, Massachusetts to the latter. Some sense of the endurance of these differences is provided in line 3, which indicates—among those who did drop out—the rate at which they have returned. While by now we are not surprised by the greater magnetism of the church is North Carolina, where two-thirds of the dropouts have returned, the fact that about half of the dropouts in both Massachusetts and California also returned reflects the residual hold the church has.

The Social Importance of Religion

In view of the strong differences revealed in Table VI–4, we are prepared for the findings of Table VI–5, which deals with the social role played by religion in the lives of these respondents. This too differs from one state to the next.

Since we have already observed in chapter 2 the strong correlation between scores on the Parish Involvement Index and the likelihood of reporting religion to be "very important in my life," it makes sense to expect those regions with high rates of parish involvement to have high rates of agreement with this sentiment. For the most part, our expectation is met here, but there is one deviation worth noting because we will encounter it in some detail soon. Massachusetts, in Table VI–4, was slightly ahead of California in terms of its residents' formal relationship with the church. In Table VI–5, however, it lags behind on the issue of religion's importance. In other words, relative to Californians, Massachusetts residents go to church more, but they regard religion as less important. Relative to Massachusetts residents, Californians regard religion as more important, but they are less involved in a parish. We will return presently to this point of more lower-key church involvement in

Table VI–5
Social Importance of Religion in Four States

	NC	OH	MA	CA
1. % Saying religion is very important in their lives	68	53	37	47
2. % Saying that other family members share their religious views	81	78	75	70
3. % Saying that close acquaintances share their religious views	68	57	51	50

Massachusetts and/or more higher-pitch religious interest unaccompanied by church involvement in California.

The second and third lines of Table VI–5 return to the regional pattern observed in Table VI–4, though it must be acknowledged that little difference seems to separate the states of Massachusetts and California on these questions of religious sharedness. What is clear is the greater amount of it to be found in North Carolina, especially among non-kin-related friends, and (again) the middle position of Ohio on all of these issues. It is already starting to show up that Californians are not so much "least religious" as they are least "conventionally" religious.

Regional Difference in Piety

What was just now referred to as lower-key church involvement in Massachusetts versus higher-pitch religious interest unaccompanied by church involvement in California can be further explored in Table VI–6.

Note first the figures on line 1, which indicate that 79 percent of North Carolinians have read the Bible at home during the past year, as compared with 69 percent of Ohioans, 41 percent of Massachusetts citizens, and 59 percent of Californians. A surprise comes in seeing the considerable difference between these last two states, since, unlike the pattern of Table VI–4, where California is less "religious" than Massachusetts, we see instead

Table VI–6
Pious Practices in Four States

	NC	OH	MA	CA
1. % Who have read the Bible at home within the last year	79	69	41	59
2. % Who pray daily	69	61	46	56
3. % Who always say grace aloud at meals	61	42	18	33
4. % Who practice a meditation technique "like those taught by Transcendental Meditation, Zen, etc."	6	11	13	21

the pattern of line 1 from Table VI–5, where Californians assigned more importance to religion than did the people of Massachusetts. Lines 2 and 3 of this table repeat this reversal:
California exceeds Massachusetts in the percentage who pray at
least daily and regularly say grace aloud at meals.

Now it might be imagined that this apparent anomaly is ow-
ing to the different ratio of Catholics to Protestants in the two
states; only a quarter of the California respondents are Catholic,
whereas nearly half (48 percent) are Catholic in Massachusetts.
Knowing these figures, one might reason that while churchgoing is commoner among Catholics, pious domestic practices are
commoner among Protestants. But this explanation is not correct; of the three practices under review here, only Bible reading
at home is assumed to be commoner among Protestants than
Catholics, but separate analysis of the adherents of these two religious traditions in the four states reveals no change in the *pattern* of differences between these two states. Thus, when in line
1 of Table VI–5 more people in California than in Massachusetts
tell us that religion is very important in their lives, they are in
part reflecting their greater rate of pious practices. So it is in Table VI–6; Californians, both Protestant and Catholic, *are* more
conventionally pious than their counterparts in the Bay State. It
remains nonetheless true that Ohioans, and especially North
Carolinians, engage in these pious practices at higher rates yet.

The fourth line of Table VI–6 carries a quite different meaning, revealing a regional variation of considerable interest: Californians meditate at three times the rate of North Carolinians
and nearly twice the rate of those in the other two states. It
might appear that because the rates are modest, they are not
very significant, but one must appreciate that the question specifically asks about meditation *techniques*, and it specifically
mentions Transcendental Meditation, Zen, etc. In other words,
it is unlikely that respondents understood the question to include the practice of silent prayer, or saying the rosary, or any
other way people might simply be "meditative." This supposi-
tion is buttressed by the fact that when Catholics and Protestants are compared across the four states, their rates are
virtually identical. The regional differences, however, remain

and, by the standard of this one pious practice at least, Californians are noticeably more religious than Bay Staters and Ohioans, and, certainly more religious than North Carolinians. Meditation is big in California.

Of course, our aim here is not to assess who is more and who is less religious. We want merely to understand four religious climates. We are finding, then, that with every step in our analysis each of the four climates is taking on more and more distinctive character.

Christian Orthodoxy in Four Regions

We come finally in this exploration to the prevalence in these religious climates of elements of Christian orthodoxy. Objections can be raised that Christian orthodoxy questions are meaningless to non-Christians, and, more subtly, that what often is called Christian orthodoxy is better called Protestant— or even evangelical Protestant—orthodoxy. Our purpose here, however, is not the resolution of theological or doctrinal disputes but simply to learn about regional differences in the rate at which people declare their assent to, or belief in, certain creedal elements that are often regarded as "orthodox." Whether they in fact *are* orthodox is not of concern to this project.

Table VI–7 reports on five such creedal elements, four of which might be thought of as positive in the sense that orthodox believers could be expected to assent to them. The fifth item, however, is heterodox, and Christian believers might be expected to *dis*agree.

As in the case of the previous table, these questions were analyzed separately for Protestants and Catholics, but, except for the latter's lower rates of believing in a literal Bible or reporting a born again experience, the state-by-state differences are found in both groups. Note that lines 1 through 4 parallel the pattern just encountered in Table VI–6: North Carolina leads the way, Ohio is next, but it is Massachusetts, not California, that is least orthodox. To repeat: This is not because Massachusetts has a higher proportion of Catholics. Or, put another way, the relatively few Roman Catholics appearing in our North Carolina sample

Table VI–7
Christian Orthodoxy in Four States

	NC	OH	MA	CA
1. % Who believe in eternal life	91	90	75	79
2. % Who believe in the devil	83	75	46	57
3. % Who agree that the Bible is the actual word of God and is to be taken literally	62	46	26	40
4. % Who report a born again experience	66	41	22	40
5. % Who believe in reincarnation	19	25	28	30

are more likely than fellow Catholics in other states to believe in eternal life and the devil, and they are more likely also to report being born again. The regional differences are real, in other words, despite denominational variation in the four regions.

It is in line 5 of Table IV–7 that we see a dramatic instance of the breadth of this regional phenomenon. Reincarnation, like the practice of meditation, can be regarded—and, by some Christians, is regarded—as heretical. Entering American religious culture not only via imported movements with roots in Hinduism but also through the popularity of New Age spiritualist notions such as channeling or mediumship, the religious conception that we have had earlier lives on earth, and will have further lives here as well, is obviously alien to what most persons raised in the Judeo-Christian tradition regard as orthodoxy. And yet, just as churches absorbed yoga classes, so too have Christians found ways to blend the doctrine of reincarnation with that of eternal life. Coherence in our system of beliefs we may strive for, but lack of consistency, it seems, is not a problem (Wuthnow 1987, 45–47). Who, after all, is in a position to declare that any pair of religious doctrines is inconsistent?[2]

---

2. It is worth noting that Protestants and Catholics in all four states alike report belief in reincarnation at rates between 26 and 31 percent. The only exception is among North Carolina Protestants (the most orthodox of our subpopulations), where the rate is 18 percent.

Territoriality in the Four States

While no claim can be made that territoriality is a religious phenomenon, it is patently obvious—especially in light of the role already shown to be played by local ties in religious matters—that how much people move around (or think of moving around) influences their religious landscape. And how much they move around is influenced by a number of factors, including their degree of territorial identification. These four states differ considerably, and interestingly, in this regard. Table VI–8 tells this story.

Consider line 1. Because California plays such a symbolic role in the mythic culture of America (Starr 1973, 1985), it seems odd that it would be fourth among these four states in its proportion of population who identify themselves regionally (in their case, as Westerners). Ohioans (as Midwesterners) are close, but noticeably different are the people of North Carolina and Massachusetts (who think of themselves, respectively, as Southerners or New Englanders). There are no doubt good historical reasons for these latter two states to figure prominently in the self-image of many of their residents. Perhaps the Midwest is itself too vast, too heterogeneous, to facilitate regional identification. California is a different scene, however, since from its earliest days as a state, the rest of America (and much of the rest of the world) have entertained rather fixed images of the Golden State. From the "forty-niners" through the "la-la land" of movies and

Table VI–8
Territoriality in Four States

	NC	OH	MA	CA
1. % Who identify themselves regionally	76	59	75	54
2. % Who were born elsewhere than their current state of residence	29	29	35	55
3. % With at least one foreign-born parent	4	4	16	15

television, from the mission-style romantic scene conjured up by *Ramona* through the health food and physical fitness craze of today, California draws people to it on the basis of these images (among other factors) even as it broadcasts yet ever new versions of these images.

Why, then, do Californians lag behind in thinking of themselves regionally? The answer is found in lines 2 and 3 of Table VI–8. Not only are the same proportion of foreign-born parental linkages to be found in California as in Massachusetts (both of which have four times the number of such linkages as North Carolina and Ohio), but also California is way ahead in terms of migrants from other states. Fewer Californians have relatives close by as a result, therefore, fewer multiple-generation families share a territory, and more of them report a desire to move from their present community (though not if this means moving to another state).

One might read the sum of the three lines of Table VI–8 as persuasive evidence that North Carolinians are most fixed in their territoriality, Californians are least, and Ohio and Massachusetts are somewhere in the middle, though these latter two states differ considerably in the ways by which they arrive there. If, as has been demonstrated already for the total sample, local ties to one's community play a role in one's religious behavior and style, then surely territoriality differences as large as these, by virtue of their impact on local ties, carry enormous consequences for personal autonomy, parish involvement, and thus disestablishment. We will observe presently how true this statement is.

A Summary

There are such things as histories, traditions, conventions, or central tendencies in culture—what we have been calling "climates." Our inquiry in this chapter thus far has focused on four states, representing four regions, and we have asked about their differing religious climates. We also looked at differences in territoriality. We need now to summarize the several dimensions of religious climates in the four regions, somewhat along the lines just provided for territoriality.

It seems obvious enough that just as North Carolina is most fixed in territoriality, so is it most fixed religiously; its climate seems to be the most coherent, most easily described. On all four dimensions—organizational involvement, social importance of religion, pious practices, and Christian orthodoxy—North Carolina is unsurpassed on any question by any other state. Ohio uniformly is next on all four dimensions and on all questions. While this leaves Massachusetts and California to hold down third and fourth places—and they are, so to speak, more alike than either resembles North Carolina—a rather consistent distinction exists between them that crops up in many different ways. It is this: There is less interest in religion in Massachusetts (a condition most people would call "greater secularization") than in California *except for traditional churchgoing*. That is to say, compared with residents of Massachusetts, Californians are somewhat more likely to have decreased their parish involvement (or dropped out altogether), but they are quite a bit more likely to assign some importance to religion, to engage in pious practices (including unorthodox meditation), and to hold more to both orthodox Christian doctrines and the one heterodox doctrine we asked about. California compared to Massachusetts, in other words, is religiously more active; it is more religiously *interested*. Having said that, however, we must remember that on all measures except heterodoxy, Ohio and especially North Carolina exhibit even more religious climates.

Regional Variation in Religious Establishment

It should be clear by now, after discussions in chapters 1 and 4, and especially in chapter 5, that we are using the term "disestablishment" here in a rather novel way. Early on we noted that since nationhood, the United States did not have in any legal sense an established church; hence disestablishment in this sense is oxymoronic. But we also noted that, first, an evangelical Protestantism prevailed through much of America's nineteenth century; then, second, from about World War I until the 1960s, a tripartite religious mood seemed to prevail. Granted, through both of these periods dissenting groups were common, many objecting strenuously to whatever was then prevailing. But a prevalence existed nonetheless. "Established" religions could thus be said to exist.

It was the prevalent, established religion of the 1920–1960 period that was assaulted by the social revolution arising in the 1960s and continuing today. It was this established religion's taken-for-granted assumptions that were challenged: for example, that "everyone" has a denominational preference; that "everyone" either goes to church or else feels some need to explain why not; that "everyone" has a right to any religious preference but also an obligation to make that preference known; that the church has standing in the community's affairs, and the community's affairs are a natural concern of the church. In brief, what was being challenged was the assumption that church involvement—in the church of one's choice, of course—was a good thing because it signified conventionality and fundamental attachment to core American values.

The question we address now is whether this challenge was issued and felt everywhere in roughly equivalent form and strength, or whether regional differences along this line can also be discerned. If the latter, are these differences linked to the regional differences in religious climates we just reviewed?

Personal Autonomy as Disestablishment

Personal autonomy, it can be argued, is a reasonable measure of the degree to which established religion (in the sense just described) is subject to *dis*establishment. In any population, that is to say, whether defined regionally as we are doing in this chapter, or by denominational family as we will come to in the next chapter, the challenge to the conventional religion prevailing before the 1960s can be estimated by the degree to which that population is low in local ties and high in its rate of adopting the alternative morality—i.e., to the degree it is high in personal autonomy.

We already know the regional differences in parish involvement, and we also know that personal autonomy is inversely related to parish involvement. It is obvious, therefore, to expect North Carolina to be lowest in personal autonomy, Ohio to be next, and Massachusetts and California to be in the high

Table VI–9
Personal Autonomy in Four States

	NC	OH	MA	CA
1. Median score on the Local Ties Index	2.82	2.73	2.67	2.52
2. Median score on the Morality Index	+1.90	+.50	−.07	+.50
3. Median score on the Personal Autonomy Index	2.49	2.81	3.57	3.39

category. Table VI–9 provides this evidence. While our expectations are upheld, there is at least one noteworthy surprise.

Lines 1 and 2 report the two pieces of information that constitute the Personal Autonomy Index. While this latter measure (line 3) follows the pattern of Tables VI–5, VI–6, and VI–7 (in which not California but Massachusetts exhibits the greatest contrast with North Carolina), this is achieved through an unusual path. North Carolina, as anticipated, is highest in local ties and most traditional in morality. Ohio is next. But the other two states come by their similar personal autonomy scores in different manner. California, it will be noted, scores lowest in local ties but resembles Ohio on the Morality Index. Massachusetts therefore ends up with the highest score on the Personal Autonomy Index because of its extreme position on the morality measure—the only state of these four with a negative median score (meaning that more of its citizens agree with the alternative outlook than with the traditional outlook). That score would be even higher if Massachusetts had local ties less like Ohio's and more like California's.

Evidence not shown here makes clear that California's median score on the Morality Index results not from a clustering around the middle range of scores, as does Ohio's median, but from a bipolar distribution of scores—many people have adopted the alternative outlook, but many are committed to the traditional views. While, compared with North Carolina and Ohio, California exhibits far more personal autonomy, it comes to its personal autonomy score in a way significantly different from Massachusetts. Of the two it is the more mobile, but also the more morally traditional, population. This may explain why the impact of personal autonomy on parish involvement is greater in California ($r = -.46$) than in Massachusetts ($r = -.38$). (In Ohio the correlation is $-.40$, and in North Carolina, $-.36$.) Whatever the truth of this surmise, however, Californians are structurally freer to follow their religious impulses than are their counterparts in Massachusetts. Put another way, the Bay State may be *culturally* less traditional than the Golden State, but residents of the latter have greater *freedom to act* on their cultural values.

The Meaning of the Church

In chapter 4 we observed that personal autonomy influences people's view of the church, rendering it less collective-expressive and more individual-expressive. We can note now that this relation is upheld in all four states. In other words, parish involvement in all four regions declines as personal autonomy increases, in part because the latter encourages a view of the church that makes involvement an individual "exchange." At the same time, it can be said that personal autonomy seems to encourage this individual-expressive view of the church irrespective of the level of parish involvement.

It is the similarity of the four states in this regard, however, not their dissimilarity, that stands out in this analysis of the relationship between personal autonomy and the meaning of the church. The point here, then, is much the same as the one made toward the end of chapter 4: The forces emerging from the sociocultural revolution begun in the 1960s—forces labeled here as personal autonomy—not only have an inhibiting effect on parish involvement but also have an effect on the very meaning of that involvement. And these effects can be seen in all four regions.

Conclusion

The dominant findings of this chapter are therefore two: 1) The regions of the United States represented in this inquiry differ considerably in both religious style and personal autonomy, and thus in the degree to which they have experienced disestablishment. 2) Irrespective of these differences, however, personal autonomy is everywhere corrosive of parish involvement and thus a force for further disestablishment, in part because it encourages a changing view of the church.

But just as states or regions differ from one another in these terms, so do denominational families differ from one another *within* states. And we know states differ in their profiles of denominations. Exploring these variations will occupy us in the next chapter.

Chapter Seven

Disestablishment in Four Regions of America

As we have had occasion to say several times already, to talk of religious "disestablishment" in modern America is to talk metaphorically; there is no establishment to disestablish, nor has there been any for nearly two hundred years. Nevertheless, at least two monumental shifts in the relationship of religion and culture—corresponding to disestablishments—have occurred in our nation's history. First, of course, was the constitutional prohibition against any federally supported church—the first disestablishment. Then, when the reality of religious pluralism in the United States was acknowledged by early in this century, and the country was recognized as no longer culturally "Protestant," a second disestablishment took place. Now, as a result of the social revolution of the 1960s and '70s, the cultural role of the church has changed again. Parish involvement has declined with increased personal autonomy, and—what is culturally more relevant—the *meaning* of that involvement has been significantly altered. Yet another step of disestablishment has taken place.

The earlier chapters of this book have shown how this change has occurred generally. In the two previous chapters the focus has been on regional religious differences, the implicit idea being that the history and current situation in each of four regions have meant that the general change has been experienced in markedly *different* ways. It is the task of this chapter to describe and document these differences.

The task is complex, chiefly because of the intermingling of region and religious denominations, both in the history of each state and in its current social life. Complicating matters further are migration patterns, noticeably different in our four states, as well as differences in the amount of "switching" from one denomination to another, also different in the four states.

We have made good use of the concept (and measure) of "personal autonomy," a general-duty concept that, on the one hand, reflects the degree of impact on people of the 1960s social revolution and, on the other hand, predicts quite well persons' level of parish involvement. Since we have seen that personal autonomy is related to denomination (chapter 4) but also to region (chapter 6), we shall, in looking simultaneously at both denomination and region, once again find the concept useful in our analysis. First, however, we look at some vestiges of the "establishment" status in the several states.

What Remains of the Second Disestablishment?

One of the ways of conceiving of the so-called second disestablishment is to see it as significantly erasing a Protestant hegemony, replacing it with a preference for everyone's religion of choice. By this standard, then, the third disestablishment replaces a preference for a religion of choice with the option of being religious in one's own way or not being religious at all. The degree to which this second disestablishment viewpoint remains can be seen in the proportion of persons who are still affiliated with the denomination in which they were raised. While such loyalty is by no means a perfect measure of involuntary or inherited religious involvement, at least it can be said that a departure from the denomination of one's childhood represents something of a voluntary view of the religious life. Table VII–1 provides the data for making several interesting observations along these lines.

A number of this table's features are worth noting:

1. It is obvious that when religious affiliation overlaps ethnic identity, the likelihood of persons' remaining in their childhood religion is considerably enhanced. This situation is clear in the case of Jews, where defection—if it occurs—is to become None. The situation with Black Protestants is no doubt similar, but documentation is complicated by our measure of the category. It consists of all persons identifying themselves ethnically as Black *and* as some kind of Protestant. The overwhelming majority of these people belong, we know, to so-called Black churches, but a few (four or five only) are affiliated with so-called White Prot-

Table VII-1

In Four States, the Percent Raised in a Denominational Family Who Remain in That Family*

Denominational Family	NC	OH	MA	CA	Average
Liberal Protestant	61 (18)	57 (49)	63 (96)	52 (75)	58%
Moderate Protestant	39 (18)	71 (143)	55 (40)	50 (104)	60%
Conservative Protestant	93 (466)	82 (196)	63 (71)	71 (151)	84%
Roman Catholic	75 (48)	80 (188)	79 (384)	71 (213)	77%
Black Protestant	93 (85)	93 (41)	82 (11)	90 (35)	91%
Jewish	(4/4)	(6/7)	81 (27)	79 (19)	82%
State average for all above families	89%	78%	73%	66%	
% Switching to another family	5	10	9	15	
% Switching to none	6	10	16	15	
% Raised none who remain none	0	2	2	4	
	100%	100%	100%	100%	

*The 39 cases of Other Religions are not included here, being too heterogeneous to analyze. Base Ns are shown in parentheses.

estant denominations. Moreover, a few Black persons in the sample who are Catholic (again, about four) are classified as Roman Catholic. Of course, it is entirely commensurate with the thesis of establishment religion being put forward here that such high rates of retention are in significant measure a function of the "involuntary" nature of ethnicity—and thus of religion.

2. Religious legacies live on in yet another way. Thus, Liberal Protestants' retention rate is highest in Massachusetts, where they once dominated the church scene. Moderate Protestants' retention rate is highest in Ohio, where they reigned supreme. And it is in North Carolina where Conservative Protestants enjoy their greatest retaining power. Roman Catholics, whose retention rate is nearly as strong as the Jews', reveal little state-by-state variation, an exception possibly being the case of California, where their retention rate is lower.

3. But the retention rate for California is lowest in nearly all the denominational families. Its overall retention average is significantly lower than the other states (with one-third defecting), while North Carolina's is significantly higher (with only one in ten defecting).

4. One cannot disconnect this North Carolina success in retaining church members from the fact that 73 percent of North Carolina's sample are Conservative Protestants, and Conservative Protestants are second only to Black Protestants in their retention rate. It is not an exaggeration to see in these data, therefore, the remains of a North Carolina "establishment" religion unlike anything found in the other three states.

5. Because of its high retention rate there remains little room for religious movement in North Carolina; defectors are essentially split between those who switched to another denominational family (5 percent) and those who dropped out altogether (6 percent). Only six persons in the sample were raised None, and half of them have since affiliated—all with Conservative Protestantism.

6. If Massachusetts still reveals the impress of "established" Liberal Protestantism, Ohio the impress of "established" Moderate Protestantism, and North Carolina, Conservative Protestantism's impress, what does California reveal? The answer is

found in the bottom lines of Table VII–1. There, in the reciprocal of the lowest of four retention rates, we see the highest rates of religious mobility: 15 percent switched loyalties, another 15 percent dropped out, and a noticeable minority were raised None and have stayed None. The picture of denominational religion in California portrayed here is the same one portrayed in both the distant and near past—considerable ferment and evidence that, in a sense, "established" religion never existed in California. This statement is relative, of course, but it is more than interesting that, just as remnants of establishment can be discerned in the other three states, in California the legacy of non-establishment is also to be seen.

On Regaining the Once Lost

Defectors exist in all denominations in all states, needless to say, so another index of the differential magnetism of churches is their success at regaining those they once lost. "Lost" here is somewhat vague, but for research purposes we define it as having answered affirmatively the following question:

> Has there ever been a period of two or more years when you did not attend church/synagogue, apart from weddings, funerals, and special holidays?

In fact 48 percent of the total sample indicated that they had, in this sense, "dropped out" or were "lost" to the church. This ranges, as might be expected, from 39 percent in North Carolina to 59 percent in California.

The question can be put, however, whether different denominations have differing success in the several states in attracting back their defectors. And if so, does this capacity, like the capacity to retain members in the first place, reflect "establishment" status once held? The answer is Yes to both questions, though the pattern is more muted than the pattern of Table VII–1. Partly this muting can be attributed to some pretty small numbers. (In North Carolina only three Moderate Protestants dropped out, but all of them returned, giving them a regaining rate of 100 percent, which overshadows Ohio's high rate for Moderate Protestants that otherwise, at 64 percent, exceeded Massachusetts's 57 percent and California's 40 percent.)

Massachusetts's Liberal Protestants' rate of regaining their "lost"—respectably higher at 57 percent than Ohio's 42 percent and California's 40 percent—is overtaken in North Carolina, but this last group consists of only ten cases. North Carolina's Conservative Protestants outshine everyone else by regaining fully 89 percent of their dropouts. Based on 189 cases, this is an astounding indication of the continued pull of establishment religion in North Carolina. Only the eleven Black Protestant defectors in Ohio (ten of whom came back) have a higher rate, while most groups do not even come close to North Carolina's Conservative Protestants in this regard.

As with dropping out in the first place, the likelihood of dropouts' *not* returning is greatest in California, where 47 percent of 360 defectors failed to return, and least in North Carolina, where only 17 percent of 226 so failed. As many studies have shown, the act of dropping out is quite common among young adults, often times reversed with marriage and especially with the appearance of young children in a marriage. That process is far more likely in North Carolina, it seems—yet another indication of that state's still-established religion.

Switching Denominations

Returning to the denominational family of one's youth after dropping out for two or more years thus occurs quite frequently. Also common is the act of switching to another denominational family, a phenomenon already explored in chapter 4. All other things being equal, such switching might be expected to follow the lines of historic "establishment," similar to the patterns of membership retention observed in Table VII–1. Thus, switchers in Massachusetts might be assumed to go disproportionately to Liberal Protestantism, in Ohio to Moderate Protestantism, etc. In fact, little or nothing of this pattern is found. It is true that in Massachusetts, Liberal Protestantism outdraws Moderate Protestantism among the switchers, while in Ohio the reverse occurs. But without doubt these modest findings are overwhelmed by the fact that, not just in North Carolina but in all four states, the vast proportion of switchers going to another denominational family (i.e., *not* dropping out altogether) have become Conservative Protestants (56 percent in North Carolina; 43 percent in Ohio; 56 percent in Massachusetts; 59 percent in California). No other family approximates such recruitment success.

There is a negative side to Conservative Protestantism's success in the switching process, however. Among those departing all other denominational families, more than half (56 percent) switch into another denomination, while 44 percent leave the church altogether. Among Conservative Protestant departures, by contrast, only a third (35 percent) switch to another denomination, which means that nearly two-thirds drop out entirely. This pattern is found to be pretty much the same in all four states. The benefit that comes from a favorable "exchange rate" with other denominational families, in other words, comes at some cost to Conservative Protestantism. Just why this is the case will be explored presently.

Migration and Disestablishment

As we have been arguing throughout this investigation, geographic mobility and all other actions that minimize local, neighborhood, and community contacts serve to make parish involvement more and more a matter of individual choice. We have also argued that, even when that individual choice is to be highly involved in a church, the *meaning* of that involvement is likely to change, becoming individual-expressive, as we called it, rather than collective-expressive.

In operation, then, disestablishment of the sort we are analyzing here is fostered to the degree local ties are loosened, whether by geographic mobility or by other means. We will be turning attention presently to the major way by which we measure this loosening—the Index of Personal Autonomy—and its relationship to region and denomination. Before taking that step, however, let us look first at a fairly crude measure of mobility—the question of whether people are living in the state of their birth or have migrated in. Granted, such a gross measure does not tell us if people might have moved to one or more other states and then moved back to their native state. Nor is this measure sensitive to the age at which migrants moved into their current state of residence. Nevertheless, the following table reveals some interesting facts about disestablishment, just by reporting the proportion of each denominational family in each of four states who are not natives of their current state.

The bottom line of this table makes clear that North Carolina and Ohio have relatively stable populations (low in-migration), Massachusetts nearly the same, but California is more than half non-native born. While these facts are not surprising, the variety of rates *within* each state yield some unexpected findings. Thus, in North Carolina, Conservative Protestants and Black Protestants show extraordinarily low rates of migrants (i.e., highly stable populations); in Ohio a low rate is characteristic of Moderate Protestants (but also Conservative Protestants and Roman Catholics); and in Massachusetts, Roman Catholics (and, to some extent, Liberal Protestants) exhibit a low rate. In California, all denominational families except the Nones are primarily migrants, suggesting again that no affiliation at all may ironically be the true "established" religion of that state.

Once again, therefore, we see evidence of vestigial established religion—whether one or another denominational family remains the domain of natives and therefore is an "inherited" affiliation, or instead relies more on attracting newcomers, who are more likely to be making an individual choice. Generally speaking, all denominations in North Carolina and Ohio are primarily native, while in Massachusetts and California they are primarily migrant (with the obvious exception of Catholics and Liberal Protestants in Massachusetts, already noted). Partly this reflects the differential rates of in-migration, California (along with other sun-belt states) being the destination of so many for so long that probably all churches there have always had more migrant than native members.

Several "pockets" of Table VII–2 stand out as contrasts with such generalizations, however. Most glaring are the Roman Catholics in North Carolina, 95 percent of whom were born elsewhere. Another is the small group of Black Protestants in Massachusetts. With only ten cases, not much confidence can

Table VII-2

Percent of Each Denominational Family in Each State Who Were Born Elsewhere*

Denominational Family	NC	OH	MA	CA	Average
Liberal Protestant	50 (20)	35 (37)	36 (72)	58 (53)	44%
Moderate Protestant	45 (11)	28 (119)	59 (29)	65 (66)	44%
Conservative Protestant	23 (452)	26 (202)	55 (82)	51 (171)	32%
Roman Catholic	95 (38)	26 (181)	21 (313)	56 (167)	35%
Black Protestant	19 (80)	45 (40)	70 (10)	61 (38)	38%
Jewish	4/4	1/6	58 (24)	80 (15)	63%
None	54 (39)	34 (65)	48 (115)	48 (125)	46%
State Average	30%	29%	36%	55%	

*Other Religions are not included, Base Ns are shown in parenthesis, and percentages are not calculated in cells with fewer than 10 cases.

be placed in their high rate of 70 percent migrant, but, as we shall see later, this fact accords with other features of that small population.

On the basis of migration data, then, we can discern the following: Conservative Protestantism remains an "established" religion in North Carolina, for both white and black Protestants. This is in striking contrast with Roman Catholicism in North Carolina, which would have to be regarded as very much "disestablished"; we have to assume that Catholics electing to be church-involved in North Carolina likely do so for individual, not collective, motives. Ohio, with the lowest proportion of immigrants, shows the least variation in its denominational families; great stability—as indicated by having native-born adherents—is shown by almost all denominations. In Massachusetts, Roman Catholicism is largely home-grown as, to a lesser extent, is Liberal Protestantism. In California, migrants predominate in all groups (except the Nones), thus providing continued evidence that its legacy is that of a fluid population.

What tentative conclusion can be drawn? While the process of disestablishment, as we use that term here, can never be complete, it appears thus far that it has gone furthest in California, gone almost as far in Massachusetts, and is observed least in North Carolina. We will, however, refine this tentative judgment in the following sections of this chapter.

Personal Autonomy and Disestablishment

Since the extended discussion of personal autonomy in chapter 4, we have recognized the sizable role that this phenomenon plays in parish involvement and related matters. It is time now to see how personal autonomy is distributed in the various denominations of the four regions, and to explore its role in the disestablishment process. We are handicapped again, as in other tables in this chapter, by small numbers of cases in some instances; nonetheless a discernible pattern exists, plus a few surprises.

At initial glance Table VII–3 appears bewilderingly complex, but in fact it tells a rather simple and compelling story. This story is best begun by looking first at the next-to-last line—the

Table VII-3

In Four States, the Percent with High Personal Autonomy (Score 4–8 on Index) in Each Denominational Family

Denominational Family	NC	OH	MA	CA	Denominational Average
Liberal Protestant	55 (20)	51 (37)	79 (71)	62 (53)	66%
Moderate Protestant	36 (11)	44 (118)	66 (29)	61 (66)	51%
Conservative Protestant	25 (449)	28 (201)	37 (81)	38 (169)	29%
Roman Catholic	65 (37)	50 (181)	56 (309)	53 (167)	54%
Black Protestant	38 (79)	60 (40)	60 (10)	34 (38)	44%
Jewish	(4/4)	(5/6)	83 (24)	87 (15)	86%
State Average (for Affiliates):	33%	46%	62%	57%	
Nones	62 (39)	75 (64)	83 (114)	84 (125)	

average percentage of parish affiliates in each state who are high in personal autonomy. We find in this row of figures the same pattern encountered already in this chapter and also in chapter 6. The pattern shows North Carolina to be significantly lower in personal autonomy than the other three states, Ohio to be somewhat higher, California higher yet, and Massachusetts the highest. The pattern in Table VII–3 duplicates the one presented at the end of chapter 6 (though there it was expressed not with percentages but with median scores). We also have nearly the same ordering of states as emerged in the previous section of this chapter, except California and Massachusetts have reversed places. This reversal also parallels the one we observed in chapter 6, where California exhibited lower rates of parish involvement than did Massachusetts, but Massachusetts fell behind California in the social importance of religion, in pious practices, and in Christian orthodoxy. It seems that these two states are about equally "irreligious," but they get to that point by different routes.

The next step in reading Table VII–3 is to glance up the columns to see the degree to which this pattern is maintained in the various denominational families, keeping in mind that small numbers of cases can render some percentages unreliable. Thus, Moderate Protestants duplicate the overall pattern very well indeed—NC, OH, CA, MA is the order. So do Liberal Protestants except in the instance of North Carolina. This "interruption" of the pattern, this unexpected high rate for Liberal Protestants in North Carolina, may be random, there being only twenty cases. But it may also reflect something peculiar to the few Liberal Protestants in North Carolina in our sample. For example, in Ohio and California only one-quarter of the Liberal Protestants are "switchers-in" (and only 17 percent in Massachusetts), while in North Carolina nine of those twenty people are switchers-in. Could it be these switchers-in who "inflate" the percentage of people with high personal autonomy? The answer is clearly Yes. Eight of the nine (89 percent) are high in personal autonomy, compared with only three (27 percent) of those raised as Liberal Protestants. Not surprisingly, therefore, these switchers-in are also better educated, have higher ranked occupations, and—though not younger—consist of fewer married persons. An informed guess, therefore, is that Liberal Protestantism serves as a destination denomination for those North Carolinians whose characteristics of low local ties and adoption of the alternative morality makes their inherited religion uncomfortable.

Consider next the Roman Catholics. They too fit the pattern—though not dramatically—except again in North Carolina, where not only is the percentage who are high in personal autonomy larger than the Roman Catholic rates elsewhere, but also largest of all denominational families in North Carolina. Something is certainly peculiar here. Moreover, there are enough cases to provide some confidence in the explanation, which is to be found back in Table VII–2, where we saw that fully 95 percent of Roman Catholics in North Carolina are not native-born but migrants into the state. How might these migrants be characterized? Relative to Catholic migrants into the other three states, those in North Carolina are largely recent movers, more youthful, female, and better educated. It would appear that North Carolina's participation in the technological revolution, which has brought population increases to Charlotte and the Research Triangle near Raleigh, Durham, and Chapel Hill, has attracted a number of persons, including some Catholics, who do not fit the religious mold of their new state. They are, for example, considerably higher in personal autonomy than other North Carolinians but also higher than fellow Catholics in the other states.

We can now look at Conservative Protestants and see that once again the overall pattern is duplicated, except for the state of Massachusetts, where Conservative Protestants appear unexpectedly low in personal autonomy. We can ask, therefore, if these 81 cases have some unusual feature that might enable us to understand why their rate would be low. The answer is again affirmative; fully 27 percent of those Conservative Protestants in Massachusetts switched from Catholicism, a rate more than twice that of Conservative Protestants in California and three and a half times the rate in Ohio. In North Carolina, only 4 of the 449 Conservative Protestants were raised as Catholics. In other words, in Massachusetts, Conservative Protestants are disproportionately ex-Catholics.

Is it this ex-Catholic feature that helps explain the lower-than-expected personal autonomy score among Massachusetts Conservative Protestants? Here, too, the answer is Yes. Among Conservative Protestants in Massachusetts who did *not* switch from Catholicism, 41 percent have a high score in personal autonomy, compared with only 27 percent of the ex-Catholics. Moreover, further analysis reveals that these transfers from Catholicism are disproportionately married women unlikely to be found in professional or managerial occupations—disproportionate, that is, to their fellow Conservative Protestants. If such characteristics are associated with low levels of personal autonomy—and Table III–5 indicated that they are—then the unexpectedly low percentage for Massachusetts Conservative Protestants is accounted for.

In the case of Jews there is little to analyze in this context because the percentage high in personal autonomy is so great that there remains no room for variation. As can be seen from the far-right column of Table VII–3 (and as was already observed in chapter 4), Jews have the highest proportion of persons high in personal autonomy, exceeding even that of the Nones. This tendency—toward low local ties and the alternative morality—appears to be characteristic of Jews in all regions.

Black Protestants yield a somewhat different situation, though they too deviate from the overall state-by-state pattern. The problem is to discern *how* they deviate. Is the personal autonomy for Black Protestants inordinately high in Ohio and inordinately low in California, thus disrupting the state-by-state overall pattern? If so, then what clues are there to account for these disruptions? The Personal Autonomy Index, it will be recalled, is comprised of persons' scores on the Local Ties Index and the Morality Index. Now, the local ties of Black Protestants are lower in all four regions than the average for that region, and this is especially the case in Ohio, which means that the higher-than-expected rate of Ohio Black Protestants' personal autonomy is somewhat attributable to low local ties. (Demographically, they are more urban, female, and least likely, in comparison with Black Protestants in other states, to belong to any voluntary association other than a church.) One possible factor to account for the anomalous pattern in California is the fact that Black Protestants are *more* traditional in moral outlook than the average for all Californians (the same is true in Massachusetts, incidentally), while in Ohio they are *less* traditional than the state's average (as are North Carolina's Black Protestants).

Of course, too, we must acknowledge that our sample contains only ten cases of Black Protestants in Massachusetts and only modest numbers in Ohio and California. Perhaps in the instance of Black Protestants outside of the South it is best to leave the puzzle of personal autonomy unsolved. What we do know is that North Carolina's Black Protestants have the highest rate of parish involvement of all groups in the four regions, that Ohio's Black Protestants are second on this score, and those in California are third. What Hart Nelsen and his co-editors wrote two decades ago of the Black church appears still to be true: "What we have here is an involuntary (or at least semi-involuntary) communal organization that resembles the phenomenon of the state church" (1971, 10). Since such comments touch on the (dis)establishment process, we shall return soon to the topic.

We have finally the Nones, who, though surpassed in personal autonomy by Jews, nevertheless are higher than all other denominational families in every state (one exception: those Catholics in North Carolina). Yet the Nones, too, come close to fitting the overall model when it comes to the prevalence of personal autonomy. Region *does* make a difference, a generalization supported by those uninvolved in any parish as well as by those belonging to one or another denomination.

Parish Involvement in the Four Regions

The argument of this book is that a disestablishment process has been taking place in America since the 1960s and '70s, that this process has come about because of radical increases in personal autonomy which have had the effect of both lowering parish involvement and changing the meaning of that involvement even where it has been maintained at a high level. In general form, this argument was advanced and documented in the first four chapters, while in the three succeeding chapters we have been looking at regional variations in the general argument.

Except for the several exceptions just reviewed, the regional variation is both pronounced and occurs pretty much in all denominational families: North Carolina reveals the lowest rates of personal autonomy and thus the lowest rates of disestablishment; Ohio is next, with Massachusetts and California—though different from each other—revealing the highest rates. Does personal autonomy translate everywhere into lower parish involvement?

The answer is Yes. Parish involvement everywhere—in all denominations in every state—declines with increased personal autonomy. A table showing rates of parish involvement in the various denominations of four states (not presented here) amounts to the mirror image of Table VII–3, therefore; where personal autonomy is high, parish involvement is low; where personal autonomy is low, parish involvement is high.

Even the apparent deviations confirm the theory. Roman Catholics are unusually high in personal autonomy in North Carolina; so are they unusually low in parish involvement when compared with other Catholics. Conservative Protestants in California are relatively high in personal autonomy, and those in Massachusetts relatively low; so are their parish involvement rates reversed. The few Black Protestants in Massachusetts are unusually high in personal autonomy; so are they unusually low in parish involvement.

Personal Autonomy and the Meaning of the Church in Four States

How about the second criterion: the changing meaning of church involvement? We have maintained all along that levels of parish involvement are not by themselves a measure of disestablishment, because in this analysis disestablishment is seen not simply as a shift in individual churchgoing behavior but rather as a shift in the cultural meaning attached to churchgoing. Decline in parish involvement may very well be a consequence of a change in the cultural meaning of churchgoing, therefore, but the latter could occur without necessarily being accompanied by the former. We saw in chapter 4 that in fact increased personal autonomy led both to a decline in parish involvement *and* to a significant shift in the meaning persons give to that involvement.

We have just noted that in all denominational families in every state, higher levels of personal autonomy are associated with lower levels of parish involvement. While this negative correlation fluctuates somewhat from one group to another, there is no discernible pattern, either by state or by denomination, to indicate how or why the corrosive effect of personal autonomy would be somewhat greater in some instances than in others. What can be reiterated, however, is that the declining parish involvement has occurred to differing degrees in different regions because personal autonomy, while everywhere corrosive, is not everywhere equally prevalent.

What, then, about the effect of personal autonomy on the *meaning* of church involvement? The overall effect, as we were just reminded, was clear enough in chapter 4, but what is the effect in the several regions? Table VII–4 provides the answer.

Table VII–4 also appears intimidating, but actually it is easy to read and tells a very consistent tale. Somewhat collapsed because we have separated the sample into four states, it is a replication of Table IV–5, which showed that personal autonomy has great impact on people's view of the church. Now we see the same tale is told in each state. That tale is this: Even while holding constant the level of parish involvement (High, Moderate, Low), those persons who are high in personal autonomy, compared with those who are low in personal autonomy, are more likely to score high on the Church as Individual Choice (CIC) Index. (Compare the first column with the second, the third column with the fourth, etc.) Put in path analysis terms, the situation in each state resembles what was found for the entire sample: Only one-third of the impact of personal autonomy on the CIC Index is mediated by parish involvement; two-thirds of the impact is direct. In other words, independent of the level of church involvement, two-thirds of the cultural meaning

Table VII–4

In Four States, the Influence of Personal Autonomy on Viewing the Church as Individual Choice

Parish Involvement	NC Personal Autonomy		OH Personal Autonomy		MA Personal Autonomy		CA Personal Autonomy	
	High	Low	High	Low	High	Low	High	Low
% Who Score High on the Church as Individual Choice (CIC) Index								
High	36	12	32	17	50	31	50	23
Moderate	48	19	65	31	60	51	70	49
Low	64	42	70	42	77	64	74	55

attached to that involvement varies according to level of personal autonomy. And personal involvement (we have argued) is a function of the degree to which the fall-out of the 1960s–'70s revolution has reached persons through reduced local ties and an alternative morality. This is true in all four states. Of the 12 comparisons possible in Table VII–4, none is "reversed." Even in the population that most critically tests the theory—the highly involved—the theory is consistently upheld.

Further Corroboration

As in chapter 4, we can corroborate the theory further by looking at friendship patterns in parishes. The argument is not that having friends in church indicates a collective-expressive view. Rather, the argument is that *not* having friends in church while still maintaining moderate or high involvement in a parish indicates an individual-expressive view. Using the same three questions employed toward the end of chapter 4:1) feel closer to fellow religionists, 2) know many at one's own church, 3) most of one's friends attend one's church—and looking at those high or low in personal autonomy among the moderately and highly involved in four states, we have 24 possible comparisons. Of these 24, only two fail to support the theory, and both occurred on the least direct question—about feeling closer to fellow religionists—and among moderately involved, not highly involved, persons.

Disestablishment in Four Regions

There would seem to be no question that in general a disestablishment process has occurred in all four regions more or less as anticipated in chapter 1 and as documented for the sample as a whole in chapter 4. The social revolution of the 1960s has led to increased personal autonomy, which has had the effect of lowering parish involvement, but, independent of that effect, it also has changed the meaning of parish involvement from collective-expressive to individual-expressive. The issue now is how the regional differences just observed reveal even more about this disestablishment process.

North Carolina is clearly the easiest to describe in these terms: Except for recently migrated Roman Catholics—and possibly a segment of Liberal Protestantism—this Southern state shows relatively little effect of the social revolution of the 1960s and '70s. Virtually no one in our sample of North Carolinians was raised outside of a denomination, and half of those few who were have since become Conservative Protestants. This state has the highest retention (i.e., denominational loyalty) rate of the four states, and the fewest who ever dropped out. Among the minority who did drop out, fully 85 percent have returned. North Carolina leads all four states in people who are high in local ties and still hold a traditional moral position on family and sexual matters. It therefore has the lowest rate of personal autonomy but therefore also the highest rate of parish involvement.

While North Carolina churches cannot be said to be insulated from the social forces that are the subject of this book (the Catholics alone demonstrate that fact), they are nonetheless in a better position to carry on as they have been doing since before the 1960s. In this sense, they have experienced least the qualitative change we are calling the third disestablishment.

Of Ohio it might be said that the church situation there resembles North Carolina's—to a lesser degree. Its "uniquely average" status is maintained on this front, as it scores somewhere in the middle between North Carolina and the other two states on every measure we have examined. The one exception even helps confirm the rule; Ohio has 1 percent fewer in-migrants than even North Carolina. While evidence of ecclesiastical change is apparent in Ohio, and it is obviously occurring at a rate faster than its Southern counterpart, nevertheless it has felt the third disestablishment only somewhat.

In disestablishment terms, Massachusetts and California are more alike than either resembles the other two states on most issues. Nevertheless, they differ considerably in how they arrive at their apparent similarity. In brief, it might be said that in Massachusetts the third disestablishment appears to have happened quickly and powerfully; in California there was little or nothing to disestablish. These are sweeping generalities, of course, but evidence tends to uphold them.

For example, in Massachusetts churches were and are the avenue by which more people express religiousness than is the case in California. More Bay Staters have remained loyal to the denominations of their childhood, fewer have dropped out for a period of two or more years, and more of those who did drop out have returned rather than switched denominational families. Perhaps of most significance, the people of Massachusetts, in all denominational families except Black Protestants (of whom there are but ten cases in the survey), are more involved in their parishes than their California counterparts. On this basis, therefore, one might say that the disestablishment process has been less pronounced in Massachusetts than in California, even as it is clearly more pronounced in both places than it is in Ohio and North Carolina.

From the California perspective, on the other hand, while the church may be less important to its citizens than to Massachusetts's citizens, religion seems to be more important. Californians claim to find religion important in both personal terms and as orthodox doctrine. They are more pious in both conventional and unconventional ways. By this reckoning, the disestablishment process would appear to be less pronounced in California. Do we have a contradiction here? Perhaps not if we look simultaneously at region and denomination.

Denominations and Disestablishment

Because of the sizable differences between regions in the relative strength of different denominations, one cannot speak of denominational variation without implying regional variation, nor can regional variation be discussed without implying denominational variation. Here, we want to look at regional differences in single denominations (or "families" thereof) to learn what we can about the third disestablishment.

Roman Catholicism

Roman Catholicism is alone among denominations in this study for having formalized the 1960s social revolution in its own way. Vatican II was both symptom and cause of massive changes in the Catholic Church, and when plans for it were undertaken, no one could have foreseen how timely the deliberations would be. In the United States a Catholic had been elected President for the first time, Catholic youth were being educated at rates commensurate with old-line Protestants, and Catholic parents were flocking out of ethnic ghettos into pluralistic suburbs. In short, Roman Catholicism had clearly joined the "mainstream." (The literature is vast, but see, e.g., Kennedy 1988; D'Antonio, et al. 1989; Greeley 1989, 1990; Seidler and Meyer 1989 for analyses of the social context of recent changes in Catholicism.) The Second Vatican Council gave voice to many of these changes.

If diminished local ties and adoption of an alternative morality are ways by which persons accommodate to modernity, and if increased personal autonomy is the product of that accommodation, and if increased personal autonomy leads to reduced parish involvement and a change-over of the church's cultural role from collective-expressive to individual-expressive, and these latter changes constitute a third disestablishment, then it can be suggested that nowhere has the jolt of disestablishment been felt more keenly than among Catholics in Massachusetts. One reason has to do with the declining link between religion and ethnicity. Granted, to be certain of this assertion we would need data from the pre-1960 period, but even without such data a convincing case can be made.

We saw in chapter 5 how, in 1916, fully 71 percent of Massachusetts's population was Roman Catholic. While that proportion declined somewhat with the turning off of the ethnic immigration valve in the 1920s, Catholicism nonetheless remained intimately interwoven with the state's ethnic structure and thus its government and politics. Indeed, Massachusetts was selected in this study as a state in which ethnicity was presumed still to dominate the religious scene, at least in Catholicism.

In fact, we find that, whatever its dominant role in religion might have been at one time, ethnicity is not a factor in the personal autonomy of current Massachusetts Catholics, and thus not much of a factor in their parish involvement. Here is the procedure used: We classified Catholics as "ethnic" if they indicated ancestral origins in French Canada, Czechoslovakia, Germany, Ireland, Italy, Mexico, or Poland. All other Catholics were deemed nonethnic. Seven out of ten Catholics in Massachusetts are ethnic by this crude scheme, but among neither the old nor the young does ethnicity influence the level of personal autonomy. The situation is much the same with respect to parish involvement; among the young, ethnics are slightly more likely (by 8 percentage points) to be highly involved, but among the old, it is the nonethnics who are (by 2 percentage points) more involved. While ethnicity clearly has not disappeared in Massachusetts, its presumed strong relationship to involvement in the Roman Catholic Church (and, by implication, the meaning of that involvement) has obviously waned.

The contrast with Ohio is striking. Ohio has an even higher proportion of ethnics among its Catholics (74 percent). Ethnicity, among both old and young, is strongly—and negatively—related to personal autonomy and thus makes sizable differences in the rates of parish involvement. (Differences are 22 and 17 percentage points respectively for old and young.) Unlike Massachusetts, then, Ohio's Roman Catholic Church seems still to be supported by networks of ethnic relationships.[1]

North Carolina has too few cases of Catholics to allow minute analysis, but while two-thirds of North Carolina Catholics are ethnic by our scheme, whether they are ethnic or not appears to make no difference to their Catholicism. (Among the young, it may even have a dampening effect on involvement; with so few cases, one cannot be sure.)

California presents a picture somewhere between Massachusetts and Ohio on this front. Ethnicity is associated with lesser levels of personal autonomy among the older Catholics, but this

---

1. Waters's interviews with white Catholic ethnics in the suburbs of the Bay Area of California and in Philadelphia lend support to this possible interpretation. "Many . . . reported growing up in an environment in which ethnic groups and the differences between them were very important. This was contrasted with the perception that their Silicon Valley or Philadelphia Main Line suburb was not the same. . . . Many of them mapped the city [of their youth] in terms of parishes." (1990, 98–99) Presumably this change is pronounced in Massachusetts but not so pronounced in Ohio.

situation is, if anything, reversed among the young. Perhaps the thesis advanced by Mary C. Waters (1990) and others is observable here—that younger generations have ethnic "options," allowing them to put on or cast off their ethnic identities in ways not open to earlier generations. If so, increased personal autonomy may be manifest in the ability to activate one's ethnicity if one chooses. Compared with the other states, however, California has significantly fewer Catholics whose ethnicity is closely linked to the Catholic Church. People whose ancestral origin is Mexico are an obvious exception, but they constitute only 6 percent of the entire California sample and only 17 percent of the Catholics in that sample.

In summary, then, Catholicism in Massachusetts appears to have been jolted the most by the third disestablishment, Catholicism in Ohio the least. North Carolina Catholics seem to resemble Massachusetts Catholics in this regard, though the small number of cases in North Carolina makes this generalization somewhat precarious. California occupies a middle position between Massachusetts and Ohio, but ethnicity in general probably structures less of California's social life, including parish life, than is found now in Ohio and used to be found in Massachusetts.

Conservative Protestantism

We have had occasion at several points so far to comment on the success Conservative Protestantism has had at maintaining membership, partly through the loyalty of those raised in this denominational family and partly through conversion. This portrait is not found to the same degree in all regions, however. It correctly depicts the Conservative Protestantism of North Carolina and, to a lesser extent, that of Ohio, but Conservative Protestantism in California and Massachusetts is far more tumultuous.

In North Carolina Conservative Protestantism is remarkably stable. Only Roman Catholics in Ohio have a lower rate of persons who have dropped out of church for two or more years. Moreover, the conservative Protestants of North Carolina exhibit the highest rate of all groups anywhere in returning to church if they did drop out and the lowest rate of dropping out permanently. All of this bespeaks a high degree of "establishment," to be sure, and it contrasts with North Carolina's Catholics and, to a lesser extent, its Liberal and Moderate Protestants.

But it also contrasts with the Conservative Protestants in the other three states, especially those in California and Massachusetts. Thus, in these states and Ohio, Conservative Protestants report having dropped out for two or more years at rates equal to those of Liberal and Moderate Protestants and higher than those of Catholics. The same can be said about the rates of dropouts who then return; they are no higher than the Liberal and Moderate Protestant rates and not as high as the Catholic rate. As for the rate of dropping out permanently, the contrast with North Carolina is striking. Table VII–5 shows these permanent dropout rates in each state for each of three denominational families. As Table VII–5 makes clear, the established position of Conservative Protestants in North Carolina is unusual for them. Elsewhere they suffer considerable attrition, just as other Protestant denominational families do. This established character in North Carolina is more nearly duplicated in Ohio, but there all denominational families have low rates.

It must be pointed out, however, that, along with its high rates of attrition in California and Massachusetts, Conservative Protestantism enjoys high rates of conversion into its ranks.

Table VII–5
By State and Denominational Family, the Rate at Which Persons Have Dropped Out Permanently

% Who have dropped out permanently among those raised as:	NC	OH	CA	MA
Conservative Protestant	5 (466)	9 (196)	21 (151)	27 (71)
Liberal or Moderate Protestant	11 (13)	8 (85)	20 (122)	21 (79)
Roman Catholic	13 (48)	8 (188)	12 (213)	13 (384)

Whereas only 4 percent of North Carolina's massive numbers of Conservative Protestants came into that family from elsewhere, that figure is one-fifth in Ohio, one-third in California, and nearly half in Massachusetts (and jumps to 54 percent among the young in Massachusetts). The point is that, in contrast to its established status in North Carolina, Conservative Protestantism is quite volatile elsewhere. It seems pretty clear, therefore, that the "meaning" of church and churchgoing in North Carolina is one thing—at least for Conservative Protestants—but it is a quite different thing in other regions; what may still be collective-expressive in the South is less so in the Midwest and has become more individual-expressive in New England and on the Pacific Coast.

For example, among Conservative Protestants in North Carolina and Ohio who are highly involved in a parish, 14 and 9 percent score high on the Church as Individual Choice (CIC) Index, as compared with 21 and 23 percent in California and Massachusetts. Among those moderately involved, the comparable figures are 25 and 29 percent for North Carolina and Ohio versus 56 and 52 percent for California and Massachusetts. While Liberal and Moderate Protestants exhibit something of the same pattern of differences between states—although at significantly higher rates—Catholics do not. The view that church is a matter of personal choice tends to increase as parish involvement decreases in all instances, but the difference between North Carolina and Ohio on the one hand and California and Massachusetts on the other is most pronounced in Conservative Protestantism.[2]

Liberal and Moderate Protestantism

Little needs to be added to the picture already drawn of Liberal and Moderate Protestantism. While these denominational

---

2. R. Stephen Warner (1988, 33–37) has made good use of Alberoni's (1984) distinction between the "nascent state" and the "institutional state" in his analysis of change in the Mendocino, CA, Presbyterian church. That distinction is not inappropriate in characterizing the difference between Conservative Protestantism in North Carolina and Ohio (where it is "institutional") and Conservative Protestantism in California and Massachusetts (where it is "nascent").

families, too, have experienced high rates of dropping out and not returning, among the baby-boom generation especially, high rates characterize the older generation as well. This suggests that the corrosive effects of disestablishment, including the shift from a collective-expressive to an individual-expressive view of the church, have been occurring in Liberal and Moderate Protestantism for a longer time than in, say, Catholicism. Interestingly, it is the remnant of these two denominational families in North Carolina (with Methodists and Presbyterians reclassified as Conservative) that constitute the exception to our generalization. The numbers are small, of course, but nonetheless telling; only in North Carolina do these two denominational families reveal high rates of conversion into the family; indeed, 35 percent of their current affiliates are converts from other families. The gap in absolute numbers between this figure and the number of Conservative Protestants is enormous, but probably it is the fact that religion in general is so "established" in North Carolina that persons dropping out of one denomination are led to join another. In other states, especially California and Massachusetts, such pressure seems not to exist. As Roof (1988b) warns, however, and as the data here on Catholics in North Carolina suggest, even North Carolina is not entirely immune to forces conducive to personal autonomy and thus to disestablishment.

Conclusion

The process of disestablishment in four regions of America might thus be summarized as follows: It has been felt least in North Carolina, somewhat in Ohio, and massively in Massachusetts. Religion in California, which entered the post-1960s period already largely disestablished, has experienced less change than Massachusetts, therefore, but only because it had been through much of the experience before. Californians continued to be the most mobile, least "churched," of our four populations, but perhaps partly for that reason there was less of a religious establishment to be jolted than could be found in Massachusetts. Ohio has been moderately successful in stemming the disestablishment tide, especially in Roman Catholicism, while North Carolina's success is notable except for Catholics.

Has there been a "third disestablishment," therefore? Such a question begs not for a yes or no answer but rather some ruminations. These ruminations will occupy the final chapter.

Chapter Eight

A Third
Disestablishment?

Throughout the preceding chapters disestablishment has been called a metaphor, since one cannot literally disestablish what has never been established. And one of the hallmarks of religion in America is that no religion was ever established; church and state were "separated."

Casual acceptance of such a generalization has led to two contradictory interpretations, however—both erroneous. One interpretation, illustrated by Jefferson's prediction that all Americans would be "unitarians" by mid-nineteenth century, errs in imagining that the disestablishment leading to separation of church from state eventuates in so much "free thought" that churches become little more than discussion groups. Such has not occurred and is unlikely, it seems, ever to occur in this country.

The other interpretation, also in error in some sense, is more subtle. It is that with the separation of church from state came the full-fledged voluntary church. For example, writing about Americans of 1800, Nathan O. Hatch says:

> What did Christian freedom come to mean for people ready to question any source of authority that did not begin with an act of individual choice? . . . In a culture that increasingly balked at vested interests, symbols of hierarchy, and timeless authorities, a remarkable number of people would wake up one morning to find it self-evident that the priesthood of all believers meant just that—religion of, by, and for the people. (1980, 547)

Hatch's own analysis of the Disciples of Christ denomination and his identification of what he calls the "irony" that a movement to tear down denominational boundaries would end up becoming a denomination make clear that the extreme populist thrust he assigns to the early nineteenth-century Christians was never complete, however; institutional trappings could not be entirely escaped.

What both of these interpretations miss is the point that people's ties to churches were never doctrinal alone and therefore never entirely voluntary; however much religious change persons may have undergone, they were never absolutely free in each generation to make their own ecclesiastical selection. Family ties especially—but also friends, neighbors, social class, and domestic status—always impinged. For some, so did ethnicity. Put another way, the so-called voluntary principle in American church life was always truer in theory than in practice.

At least until recently. Just as the first disestablishment made possible a theretofore-unheard-of religious freedom, and just as the second disestablishment deprived Protestantism of its place of honor, so has the social revolution of the 1960s and '70s wrought a major change: a near absolute free choice in the religious marketplace. This change we have been calling the third disestablishment, and it has taken place primarily because of the greatly increased personal autonomy Americans now experience.

What is the larger meaning of this third disestablishment? Here in this concluding chapter we want to speculate about that question in three different ways. First, on what basis can the change we have been analyzing be regarded as a major or qualitative change? Second, what are some social consequences of this change? And, finally, what does this change tell us about religion in modern-day America?

The Case for a Qualitative Change

What makes the third disestablishment a qualitative change and not simply an intensification of the continuing process it undoubtedly reflects? Several responses are in order:

1. By various measures, the centuries-old pattern of increasing church membership and attendance seems to have peaked in the 1960s. "Seems" is a necessary word to use here because answering the question of church growth or decline is a good deal more difficult than asking it. Not only are there regional and denominational differences of considerable magnitude (and contradictory direction), but also populations change size, and denominations change boundaries. Nonetheless, the long-term

process by which an ever-increasing proportion of Americans affiliated with some religious organization appears to have at least reached a plateau if not peaked and declined. It may, moreover, be more than coincidence that the periods of the first and second disestablishments were also periods of plateau or decline. They proved to be temporary, it is true, and so might the current trend be reversed and the "churching" of America resume. But even were such a reversal to occur, the period of 1960–1990 might still be regarded as a third disestablishment on the grounds that as in the previous two cases of disestablishment, a significant change occurred in the relationship between church and culture.

2. A second sign of a qualitative change is found in the nature of this changing relationship between church and culture. In the preceding chapters we have referred to this change as the shift in the meaning of the church from that of a collective-expressive agency to that of an individual-expressive agency. Greater numbers of persons now, we said, legitimately look upon their parish involvement as *their* choice, to be made according to *their* standards. That involvement is now calculated as rewarding or not by individually derived equations. "Church" is no long "inherited." What this means to parishes is not only a weakening of denominational loyalties but also the foreknowledge that any change of programming undertaken to please one sector of the clientele is possibly going to displease another sector. It is not that individual churches cannot or will not grow, but any growth is likely to come at some cost—at the very least, in the displeasure to be felt by the long-term members of the growing parish as it undergoes change.

3. This latter possibility is but one instance of a larger phenomenon making for a third disestablishment. Reference is to the irony of the voluntary church's becoming so voluntary that it can no longer mediate or channel collective interests. Surely to the degree this is happening we are observing a change in the relationship between church and culture, a change, moreover, that is the "dark" side of the otherwise applauded escalation in individual choice. As Michael Harrington writes, "Political theology rightly understands that privatization is the great enemy

of religion in the modern world—not, as some sociologists think, its salvation" (1983, 206). In this regard, Harrington joins with Bellah, et al. (1985) and—well before that—Nisbet (1953) in bemoaning the shrinking role of churches and other "communities of memory" or "redemptive institutions" in powerful civic affairs. It is not at all clear, however, that the situation can be otherwise. Personal autonomy is not increasing simply because individuals are demanding more of it; to a significant degree personal autonomy is also thrust on people in certain situations, whether desired or not. Since the church decreasingly commands their loyalty, therefore, and since fewer parallel loyalties such as kinship or territorial ties exist to encourage church involvement, the church is disempowered. It cannot deliver the votes, so to speak.

Just as the first and second disestablishments restructured the relationship between church and culture, so has that relationship been restructured yet again as a result of the social revolution taking place in the last third of this century. Increased individual rights, whether sought out or exercised by default, cannot be translated by churches into political leverage. This situation should be kept in mind as the "new Christian right" makes its assault on religious liberty. It is not that danger is nonexistent on that front, but that insofar as it is dangerous, it emanates not from churches but through secular politics. As Tocqueville so plaintively warned, democracy—and with it, individual religious liberty—can easily become a tyranny by the majority unless certain countervailing forces are at work. Among these could be counted what we have called here the "inheritability" of parish involvement and the degree to which it therefore could express collective commitments transcending the parish. The research reported here suggests a significant decline in this process.

4. Final evidence that a qualitative change has occurred can be drawn from the fact that while regions and denominations differ in *how much* personal autonomy they have experienced, the *effect* of increased personal autonomy is everywhere the same. It leads to decreased parish involvement and a change from people's view of the church as a collective-expressive

agency to a view of the church as an individual-expressive agency. Invoking an idea along the lines of Max Weber's concept of "rationalization," we might speculate, therefore, that—whether or not future parish involvement rates accelerate—the meaning of that involvement has forever been individualized. Individual religious liberty, in this special sense at least, is now virtually "complete."

Perhaps it is this aspect of disestablishment—the increase in individual religious liberty whether intended or not—that makes the Roman Catholic case, especially in Massachusetts, so vivid. Obviously many church officials are disturbed by what they observe in the way of religious change and, through appeals and demands, attempt to stop it, or at least slow it down. But as this study and others (esp. Greeley 1989, 1990) suggest, irrespective of what happens to Roman Catholic parish involvement, the *meaning* of that involvement has probably been irreversibly altered.

And the Consequences?

The consequences of increasingly individualized parish involvement are many and varied. One consequence is the fading away of churches as automatic social centers for neighborhoods and small towns, their role instead becoming increasingly providers of services to individuals and family units.[1]

Needless to say, the transition we are describing does not mean that friendships are unavailable in parishes. What it does mean is that having church-related friends is not culturally expected in the manner common thirty or forty years ago. One interesting manifestation of this changed phenomenon is found in

---

1. A good prediction based on this generalization is that the decline in parochial school enrollments by Catholics has therefore been greater in Massachusetts than in Ohio. Greeley (1976, 9) reports a decline nationally of 24 percent from 1965 to 1975, but surely there are regional differences. If the theory here is correct, it leads to the above prediction because personal autonomy rates are higher in Massachusetts than in Ohio. Despite generous efforts by personnel in the National Catholic Education Association in Washington, I was unable to get the data necessary to test the prediction. Not only is the "take rate" difficult to gauge without an eligible population to compare with an enrolled population, but increased use of parochial schools by non-Catholics complicates even the accuracy of an enrolled population.

Conservative Protestants' responses to the question of whether they feel closer to fellow members of their denomination. Among those highly involved in a parish in North Carolina we might expect the highest rate of affirmative response. Instead we observe the lowest among Conservative Protestants in the four states (54 percent vs. 71, 63, and 66 percent in Ohio, Massachusetts, and California). Why would this be? In North Carolina most people one encounters in *or* outside of one's church are likely to share one's Conservative Protestant outlook if not one's inherited denomination. In the other states people are more likely to *choose* both their denomination and their friends, making both choices on an individual basis. Interestingly, this counterintuitive pattern is found also among highly involved Roman Catholics. In Massachusetts, where Catholic involvement preserves some of its "inheritability," the rate of feeling closer to fellow Catholics is only 32 percent, as compared with 60, 53, and 47 percent among Catholics in California, Ohio, and North Carolina. Friendships, to repeat, are not precluded in the individual-expressive church, but there they are more likely to be individually derived.

Nor does this pattern contradict the findings, now quite widespread, that people join and maintain involvement in religious organizations less because of doctrinal attraction than because of social networks of which they are part. Such avenues of attachment are no less voluntary and individually motivated for being social.

A second consequence of the third disestablishment is the bureaucratization of church organization as it tries with maximum efficiency to reach its multiple aims. Following in the path of commercial enterprises, churches must try to assess the desires and tastes of their current and potential clientele, they must advertise, and they must otherwise be sensitive to themselves as deliverers of services. Such an orientation is in some sense contrary to the ethos of churches as mediators of the transcendent. As Bryan Wilson puts it: "The patterns of affective neutrality, role specificity, performance expectations, self-orientation, and even universalism, which characterize the dominant organizational mode of Western society, are all, in greater or lesser degree, alien to religious institutions, roles, relationships, and values" (1968, 428). If this characterization is correct, then we can venture the guess that the "alien" feeling is less in the Conservative Protestant churches of North Carolina, more in the churches of all denominational families in Massachusetts and California, and somewhere in between in Ohio.

A third consequence is related to the second. Recall the discussion in chapter 1 about the two kinds of identity—primary and secondary. Primary identity, we said, is reasonably permanent and unavoidable; secondary identity is put on and taken off as circumstances change. With the shift toward bureaucratization and the individual-expressive mode, churches, it can be assumed, provide less and less primary identity for people, replacing it—if identity is provided at all—with some kind of secondary identity. One's religion is voluntary not just in the sense that one can choose *what* it will be, but also in the sense that one can choose *when* to invoke it. Here again Catholicism provides the clearest illustration with the dropping off of vocations for the priesthood on the part of young men. A particularly interesting parallel is found in the growing number of women administering parishes for which bishops have insufficient priests (Wallace 1991). While our data provide no direct evidence on such subtle issues as personal identities, certainly reasonable inferences can be drawn about persons whose parish involvement is regarded by them as entirely a matter of their choice.

Still another consequence of the third disestablishment is found in the church and state arena. Generally, it might be said, claims to ever-increasing individual expressions of religion have been met by government's expanding notions of constitutionally protected religious liberties. With only a few reversals, the U.S. Supreme Court's record of "free exercise" decisions is a record of broader and broader acknowledgment that individuals, not society, define their own religion (Reichley 1985, 134).

The inevitable corollary is that many of those situations where society assigned fixed or "established" religious meaning are now regarded by courts as unconstitutional on "no establishment" grounds. It is no surprise, therefore, to find that the Warren Court that allowed conscientious-objector status on free exercise of religion grounds to self-proclaimed nonreligious persons (*U.S. v. Seeger* 1965; *Welsh v. U.S.* 1970) is the same court that at nearly the same time ruled that the school-led recital of the blandest of all possible prayers was an improper establishment of religion by the state (*Engel v. Vitale* 1962). Even where an obvious establishment practice is permitted to continue, as in the erection of a crèche scene on city-owned property (*Lynch v. Donnelly* 1984), the court concluded that the religious significance of the symbol had waned to a point where the Christ-child and manger were seasonally on a par with Rudolph the reindeer. In other words, individually chosen religious expressions enjoy expanded protection that collectively chosen religious expressions do not, at least without becoming trivialized. (This generalization is severely challenged by the 1990 case from Oregon dealing with the restrictions on peyote use by Native Americans [*Employment Division* v. *Smith*].)

This capacity of individualized religion to gain recognition by the state is in sharp contrast with two other arenas in which "establishments" have been challenged by bursts of personal autonomy: education and, to a lesser degree, healing. Certainly numerous claims are made in the name of both self-help efforts and help efforts offered by alternative deliverers in these two spheres, but, unlike the situation in the religious sphere, these efforts largely go officially unrecognized. To some extent alternative healing strategies might be said to have invaded orthodox biomedicine (McGuire 1988), and some of the independent agencies for delivering these alternative healing strategies have achieved recognition—in medical insurance plans, for example. But certification that learning has taken place and competence achieved is still primarily a monopoly of schools widely acknowledged and licensed *as schools.*

The contrast between religion and education (and to some extent the contrast between religion and healing) is thus great, and observing how schools and education (or health delivery systems and healing) are little changed institutionally from decades ago simply highlights how much has changed in churches and religious involvement. In this regard, what has happened in religion is more closely paralleled by developments among white ethnics, a comparison discussed in chapter 1. The religious change has not occurred equally everywhere to everybody, of course, but where it has occurred, a change has been felt both in individuals' relationship to churches and in churches' relationship to culture.

Disestablishment as Secularization

It is nowadays better to conceptualize religion as a cultural resource . . . than as a social institution. As such, it is characterized by a greater degree of flexibility and unpredictability. For the decline of the great religious monopolies in the West has been accompanied by the sporadic deployment of religion for a great variety of new purposes. Religion can be combined with virtually any other set of ideas or values. And the chances that religion will be controversial are increased by the fact that it may be used by people having little or no connection with formal religious organizations. The deregulation of religion is one of the hidden ironies of secularization. (Beckford 1989, 171–72)

Does the third disestablishment represent another step in the direction of secularization? The answer is almost certainly Yes, though, as commonly occurs in the secularization debate, argument can be found on both sides. There is, first off, the position taken by Bryan Wilson that secularization equals "decline of community" (1982, 154–55), and the thesis advanced here assuredly rests in part on diminished ties to community. There is, second, the notion articulated most forcefully by Peter Berger (1967, chap. 6) that the pluralization of religions leads to the implausibility of each religion and thus to secularization. Without doubt, the kind of individual choice in religious matters that we have been reviewing here represents an almost infinite permutation of religious outlooks and thus intense pluralism. Rationalization, too, is often offered as a component of secularization, and, whether from the perspective of the church or of church consumers, the kinds of means-ends calculations meant by the term "rationalization" are the calculations we have been observing in these late-twentieth-century Americans.

It is perhaps only secularization as "differentiation," a position associated with Parsons (1963) and Bellah (1964), where some ambiguity arises as to whether another step toward disestablishment is another step toward secularization. That is because the individual-expressive church is at once an agency amenable to—if not capable of—custom-fitting everyone's religious size, while at the same time it performs this function across ever more selective areas of life. That is to say, religion can be important to individuals (thus lending it sacredness) but not if it is the persons themselves who decide it is important (thus rendering it secular). As a result, we see increasingly the link between religion and society mediated through individual demand, and we see decreasingly the link between religion and individuals mediated through society's demand. Among other things, this changeover means that religion can be the source of disorder and not just of order, the view predominating before the third disestablishment (Beckford 1989, 12).

Robert Bellah has put the issue in his usual blunt terms:

> In spite of the erosion of a deep sense of religious community in much of American society, the churches and synagogues continue to be among the most important of the voluntary associations to which such large numbers of Americans belong. . . . Indeed, religious groups and societies derived from them are among the most important of the intermediate associations that exist between individual Americans and the state. If they become severely fragmented and increasingly privatized, [however,] the result will be not only the loss of a coherent religious tradition but the weakening of a democratic form of life. Should loose-boundedness triumph completely, the ground will be prepared for administrative despotism, since only the state will be left to control the atomized individuals. (1987, 229)

The increase in personal autonomy documented here, therefore, and its effects in both reducing religious participation and changing the meaning of that participation signal yet another change in the relationship between church and culture in America. If, as Robert Handy (1984, 184) argues, the second disestablishment meant that "the voluntary effort to maintain a Protestant America had failed," then the third disestablishment signals a correlative fact: Protestant churches are losing not just their leadership role with respect to American core values, but they—along with all other religious organizations—are losing the custodianship of whatever remains of American core values.

It is not that Protestant America has disappeared, then, but that religious individualism is triumphing over collective religious values of any stripe. Tocqueville feared such an outcome, though his analysis of the America of the 1830s saw the voluntary church as a major bulwark against it. Whatever the likelihood of a resulting "tyranny of the majority," therefore, the churches of the United States will be neither the avenue of that tyranny nor any longer a major defense against it.

Appendix A

The Weekly Calendars of Riverside Church, New York City, and the Crystal Cathedral, Garden Grove, California

Following is the bulletin insert from Sunday, October 14, 1990, at Riverside Church in New York City. A number of continuing activities—such as the homeless shelter, food pantry, clothing service, counseling center, and English language classes—are not included, thus making the near-continuous use of the church's facilities less obvious than it otherwise would be. Of course, Riverside Church is famed for its breadth of program, and its calendar cannot be regarded as typical.

Also included are pages from Robert Schuller's Crystal Cathedral News of January 27, 1991, announcing various activities of that church.

This Week at the Riverside Church
(October 14–October 21, 1990)

Riverside welcomes visitors and members to participate in events listed here.

SUNDAY, October 14

12:15 p.m.   We invite all visitors to have coffee in the cloister lounge, one floor below the nave, where you can meet Riverside members and learn more about church programs and activities.

A tour of the church will begin in Christ Chapel, opposite the nave, following the service of worship.

The Visitors' Center, in south hall lobby, provides information about Riverside as well as cards, gift items, records, C.D.s, pamphlets and books. Sermon and full-service audio cassettes may be ordered from the Visitors' Center or purchased at the coffee hour. To order by mail, forms are available from the racks at the cloister desk or the Visitors' Center. Allow 4 weeks for delivery.

The Tower and Carillon are closed to visitors during the first phase of the tower elevator renewal project.

THE CHURCH SCHOOL AND YOUTH DEPARTMENT AT RIVERSIDE
The Church School and Youth Department are for family members and friends of Riverside ages 6 months to 18 years. This year's curriculum explores the New Testament gospels through art, crafts, drama, trips, discussions and Bible study. Classes are taught by trained volunteers and interns from Union Theological Seminary. Register any Sunday: Nursery/Kindergarten, 6th floor MLK; elementary grades, 4th floor MLK; high school, 3rd floor MLK; stop by Coffee Hour for information or call ext. 146, weekdays.

Pre-school and elementary aged children whose parents attend worship are welcomed in Church School during the Sunday service. School registration is required.

Parents and children are encouraged to worship together in the nave on Sunday mornings. Please be seated no later than 11:00 a.m. Try to sit in the front of the nave so your child(ren) can see.

Buffet dinner is served in the south hall until 2:30 p.m. Full-course meal, $5.80.

The Cloister Library is open Sundays, 9:45–10:45 a.m. and after worship service until 3:00 p.m. Suggested readings for this week: *In The Steps of St. Paul*, by H. V. Morton; *The Joy of the Only Child*, by Ellen Peck; *The Vanishing Land*, by Robert West Howard; *Whose Little Boy Are You?*, by H. H. Brown; *Silent Spring*, by Rachel Carson.

Persons interested in individual spiritual guidance, participation in group experience, meditation training, contemplative prayer and devotional exercises may contact Rev. Fanny Erickson, ext. 242.

The Pastoral Counseling Center offers individual, marital and family therapy on a sliding-scale basis. Call ext. 250.

12:30 p.m.   SOCIAL SERVICES TRAINING SESSION, 16T. See "The Next Weeks."

12:30 p.m.   MARANATHA AIDS AWARENESS SEMINAR, 14T. See "The Next Weeks."

1:00 p.m.   "VARIETIES OF CHRISTIANITY," 12T. See "The Next Weeks."

2:00 p.m.   ECOLOGY TASK FORCE REGULAR MONTHLY MEETING, room 240 MLK.

2:30 p.m.   MEMORIAL SERVICE FOR STANFORD DEVEAUX, Christ Chapel.

3:00 p.m.   CARILLON RECITAL by Joseph Clair Davis, carillonneur.

4:00 p.m.   CHINESE CHRISTIAN FELLOWSHIP, Chapel of the Cross.

MONDAY, October 15

6:00 p.m.   WEEKDAY PRAYER AND MEDITATION SERVICE, Christ Chapel.

7:00 p.m.   ALCOHOLICS ANONYMOUS, 703T.

TUESDAY, October 16

10:00 a.m.   THE MEMORIAL SOCIETY, room 537. Call ext. 218 for an ap-
3:00 p.m.   pointment.

4–7:00 p.m.   HOMEWORK HELPERS PROGRAM FOR GRADES 6–12, 7 T. Call ext.
               147, weekdays to register or to tutor.

6:00 p.m.   WEEKDAY PRAYER AND MEDITATION SERVICE, Christ Chapel.

7:00 p.m.   NARCOTICS ANONYMOUS, 703T.

7:45 p.m.   RIVERSIDE BUSINESS AND PROFESSIONAL WOMEN'S CLUB, "Tra-
               ditional and Cross-Cultural Influences: A Japanese Quilt-
               maker in the U.S.A." All interested persons are invited,
               assembly hall.

WEDNESDAY, October 17

10:30 a.m.   OLDER ADULT FRENCH CONVERSATION CLASS, 703T. Taught by
               B. Jones.

12:30 p.m.   OLDER ADULT CREATIVE WRITING CLASS, 701T. Taught by Mary
               Stavrou.

6:00 p.m.   WEEKDAY PRAYER AND MEDITATION SERVICE, Christ Chapel.

7:00 p.m.   GULF CRISIS STUDY SERIES, 9T. "Interfaith Perspectives of Mid-
               dle East Conflicts". See "The Next Weeks."

8:00 p.m.   ADULT CHILDREN OF ALCOHOLICS (ACOA), 703T.

THURSDAY, October 18

10:00 and   OLDER ADULT ART OF MOVEMENT CLASS, 411 MLK. Taught by
11:00 a.m.   Eileen Jones.

2:00 p.m.   TOWER LEAGUE, assembly hall, "Music: A Medium for Heal-
               ing," Dr. Henry Millan, Jr., pastoral psychologist/
               minister.

4–7:00 p.m.   HOMEWORK HELPERS PROGRAM FOR GRADES 6–12, 7T. Call ext
               147, weekdays to register or to tutor.

6:00 p.m.   WEEKDAY PRAYER AND MEDITATION SERVICE, Christ Chapel.

7:00 p.m.   ALCOHOLICS ANONYMOUS, 703T.

7:00 p.m.   MEN'S CLASS BIBLE STUDY, 8C. All are invited to attend.

FRIDAY, October 19

6:00 p.m.   WEEKDAY PRAYER AND MEDITATION SERVICE, Chapel of the Cross.

7:00 p.m.   FRIDAY NIGHT YOUTH PROGRAM, assembly hall level game room. Register at the desk in the cloister or call ext 147, weekdays.

SATURDAY, October 20

9:00 a.m.   MARTIAL ARTS CLASS FOR ADULTS AND TEENS, gymnasium, sponsored by the Youth Department. Call ext. 147, weekdays, for information.

SUNDAY, October 21

5:00 a.m.   BROADCAST OF October 14 SERVICE OF WORSHIP, 106.7 FM.

8:30 a.m.   MEDITATION AND MUSIC, Meditation Chapel.

9:00 a.m.   EUCHARIST AND LAYING ON OF HANDS, Meditation Chapel.

9:00 a.m.   INTERCESSORY PRAYER GROUP, 9T library.

9:30 a.m.   CHURCH SCHOOL. For children, youth and parents. Nursery/Kindergarten, 6th floor MLK; elementary grades, 4th floor MLK, and senior high, 3rd floor MLK.

9:30 a.m.   CHURCH SCHOOL PARENTS' DISCUSSION, room 417 MLK.

9:30 a.m.   OPEN DISCUSSION ADULT BIBLE STUDY, 9T Library. Rev. Diane Lacey Winley leads on: Deuteronomy 34:1–12; Psalm 135:1–14; Phillipians 4:1–19; Matthew 22:1–14.

9:30 a.m.   NEW TESTAMENT QUESTERS CLASS, 10T. Austin Ritterspach leads on "The Pastoral Epistles: I, II Timothy, Titus."

10:45 a.m.   SERVICE OF WORSHIP, nave. Dr. Allan A. Boesak preaching. "On Staying on as a Stranger." Genesis 26:1–6; 18–25; Hebrews 11:1–14.

This Week at the Crystal Cathedral, Garden City, Calif.

SUNDAY, January 27

Nursery and Sunday School (Birth through Sixth Grades)— Nursery begins at 7:30—Sunday School 8:30, 9:30 and 11:00 a.m.

Continental Breakfast—8:00 am to 12:30 pm, Fellowship Hall.

Sunday School for Youth—9:00 am: Junior High, Room 221; High School, Room 220. 9:30 am: College/Career, Room B-22. 10:00 am: "What-sup" for Junior High, Room 221; 11:00 am, church together. Meet in west balcony.

Adult Bible Class—10 am in the Arboretum.

Women in the Marketplace—11 am to 12 pm on the 12th floor, Tower of Hope.

Conquering Compulsive Behaviors—11 am, Cathedral Concourse, Room 105.

Christian Drama Class—11:00 am, eleventh floor, Tower of Hope.

Positive Christian Singles— 10:15 am; Family Life Center; Room 120.

Conquering Codependency—11:00 am. tenth floor, Tower of Hope.

Career Builders' Workshop—10:45 am, second floor, Tower of Hope.

Evening Worship—6:00 pm in the Crystal Cathedral.

MONDAY, January 28

Stretch and Walk Time for Women—9:00 to 10:00 am, Arboretum.

Cancer Conquerors—7:00 pm, Room 120, Family Life Center.

Laubach Way to English Tutoring—9:30 to 11:30 am and/or 7 to 9 pm. Room 230, Family Life Center.

TUESDAY, January 29

Women's Bible Study—9:00 am in the Arboretum with Susan Wood. Child care available.

Positive Christian Singles—7:00 pm, Family Life Center, Room 121.

Men at Peace—7:00 pm, Family Life Center, Room 231.

Gambler's Anonymous—7:00 pm, tenth floor, Tower of Hope.

Smoker's Anonymous—11:30 to 1:00 pm, Family Life Center, Room 121.

Victors—See ad under new Support Group.

Leahs—Women overcoming anger and depression—7:00 pm, Family Life Center, Room 200.

WEDNESDAY, January 30

Men's Bible Study—7:00 am, second floor, Tower of Hope.

Wednesday Service—Open to the public, 8:30 am, Family Life Center, Freeland Hall.

Laubach Tutoring—9:30 to 10:30 am, and/or 7:00 to 9:00 pm, Family Life Center, Room 230.

Highschool—7:00 pm. Family Life Center, Room 121. (Call 971-4180 for details. Volleyball, basketball, air hockey, ping-pong and pool tournaments plus weight room will be open. Taco Bell, 9:00 to 9:30. (call for details).

Conquering Fear of Success—7:30 pm, Family Life Center, Room 121.

Alcoholics Anonymous—A 12-step program for individuals who want to live free of their alcohol addiction. Meets at 7:00 pm in the Tower of Hope, tenth floor.

THURSDAY, January 31

Overeaters Anonymous—6:30 pm. Women's Lounge.

College/Career—Open gym time—basketball, volleyball, and more! 7:00 pm. Regular meeting—7:45 pm, Room B20/22.

Stretch and Walk Time for Women—9:00 to 10:00 am in the Arboretum.

Women Who Love Too Much!—7:00 pm, eighth floor, Tower of Hope.

Cocoon—(Children of Abuse Can Overcome Obstacles Now)—a unique support group for parents whose children have been abused meets at 7:00 pm in the Family Life Center, Room 221.

FRIDAY, **February 1**

Al Anon—A 12-step recovery program for *families dealing with alcoholism.* Meets at 8:00 pm, FLC, Room 231.

Junior High, Open Gym—6:30 to 7:30 pm.

F.N.L.—(Friday Night Live) for Junior High, 7:30 pm.

SATURDAY, **February 2**

Overeaters Anonymous/H.O.W.—7:30 pm, Women's Lounge.

NEW SUPPORT GROUP BEGINS THIS WEEK

Victors—(Victims of Incest Changing Their Outlook, Re-emerging with Self-Esteem), a support group for women who have been sexually abused as children, will begin a new 10-week session on Tuesday, January 29, 1991, at 7:15 pm in the Family Life Center, Room 121.

The Interview Schedule

Values and Belief Study
September, 1988
350–1000

Interviewer Name:_____ Date:_____ I.D._____ (1–4)

Tel. Number:(_____)_____   State: No. Carolina 1
California. 2   (5)
Ohio. 3
Massachusetts. 4

ELIGIBLE RESPONDENT AGREES TO ANOTHER INTERVIEW: YES NO

Hello, this is _____with FG*I Research, a national opinion center. We are conducting a nationwide study on topics of current interest. In this household I need to speak with a male/female between the ages of 25 and 60. Is (that you?) he/she available?

GET PROPER RESPONDENT ON PHONE. REINTRODUCE STUDY AS NECESSARY.

DO NOT ASK: RESPONDENT IS   Male. 1   (6)
Female 2

Before we begin, I need to know in what year you were born?

19_____

(7–8)

INTERVIEWER: IF RESPONDENT NOT BORN BETWEEN 1928 AND 1963, CONFIRM AGE AS 25 TO 60 OR TERMINATE.

I'd like to ask you a few questions about religion.

PART I

1. In what religion were you raised? RECORD VERBATIM.
    IF MORE THAN ONE: Which religion did you identify with most?

    RECORD VERBATIM: _____   (9–11)
    IF NONE: GO TO Q.2

185

1a. IF PROTESTANT: What specific denomination is that, if any?

RECORD VERBATIM._____   (12–14)

1b. IF JEWISH: Were you raised . . . READ.

> Orthodox. 1
> Conservative 2
> Reform 3   (15)
> Or none of these? 4

2. And what is your religious preference now? RECORD VERBATIM.
    IF SAME, RECORD "SAME".
    IF MORE THAN ONE: Which religion do you identify with most?

RECORD VERBATIM: _____   (16–18)

IF NONE: GO TO Q.3

2a. IF PROTESTANT: What specific denomination is that, if any?
     RECORD VERBATIM. IF SAME, RECORD "SAME."

_____   (19–21)

2b. IF JEWISH: Is that . . . READ:

> Orthodox. 1
> Conservative 2
> Reform 3   (22)
> Or none of these? 4

IF ANSWERS TO Q.1 AND Q.2 ARE DIFFERENT; GO TO Q.4.
IF ANSWERS TO Q.1 AND Q.2 ARE THE SAME, CONTINUE:

3. Have you ever been anything other than
    (PREFERENCE INDICATED IN Q.2)?
    > Yes. 1
    > No. . . . . 2 GO TO Q.5   (23)

IF NO RELIGION IN Q.1 TO 3: GO TO PART II.

4. I'd like to go over your religious preferences since you were raised as a
    (PREFERENCE INDICATED IN Q.1). Starting when you were 16 years old,
    what else have you been? Please tell me in order, earliest first.

FIRST RELIGION NAMED: _____   (24–26)

4a. How old were you when you became a FIRST RELIGION ABOVE?

Age _____

(27–28)

    PROBE: Have you been any other religion? IF NO, GO TO Q.5.

4b. IF YES: SECOND RELIGION NAMED: _____ (29–31)

    How old were you when you became a SECOND RELIGION ABOVE?

Age _____

(32–33)

    PROBE: Have you been any other religion? IF NO, GO TO Q.5.

4c. IF YES: THIRD RELIGION NAMED: _____ (34–36)

    How old were you when you became a THIRD RELIGION ABOVE?

Age _____

(37–38)

5. Would you call yourself a strong (CURRENT PREFERENCE FROM Q.2) or
not a very strong (CURRENT PREFERENCE)?

> Strong. 1
> Not very strong. 2 (39)
> (VOLUNTEERED) SOMEWHAT STRONG 3

6. Would you say you feel pretty close to other (CURRENT PREFERENCE
FROM Q.2) in general, or that you don't feel much closer to them than to
other people?

> Feel closer 1
> Do not feel closer 2 (40)
> (VOLUNTEERED) FEEL CLOSER TO OTHER PEOPLE 3

7a. Are you a member of a church/synagogue?

> Yes. 1
> No . . . . 2 GO TO Q.8 (41)

7b. How important would you say this particular congregation is in your
life? Would you say it is . . . READ:

> Very important 1
> Fairly important 2 (42)
> Or not very important?. 3

7c. Is this congregation growing in membership, or is it declining?

        Growing 1
        Declining. 2   (43)
      (VOLUNTEERED) STAYING ABOUT THE SAME 3

7d. Is the church/synagogue in the downtown of a city, in a suburb, in a small town, a rural area, or where?

        Downtown of a city 1
        Suburb 2
        Small town. 3   (44)
        Rural area 4
        Other (SPECIFY)

        _____ 5

8. How often do you attend religious services?
   (PROBE USING CATEGORIES, IF NECESSARY.)

        More than once a week. 1
        Once a week 2
        Two or three times a month. 3
        Once a month. 4   (45)
        Less than once a month 5
        Hardly ever, except holidays 6
        Never 7

9. When you were young, say 8 or 10 years old, how often did you attend Sunday school or church/synagogue? (PROBE USING CATEGORIES, IF NECESSARY.)

        More than once a week. 1
        Once a week 2
        Two or three times a month. 3
        Once a month. 4   (46)
        Less than once a month 5
        Hardly ever, except holidays 6
        Never 7

9a. What about when you were older—in your early 20s, say. How often did you go then?

        More than once a week. 1
        Once a week 2
        Two or three times a month. 3   (47)

Once a month. 4
Less than once a month 5
Hardly ever, except holidays 6
Never 7

10. Has there ever been a period of 2 years or more when you did not attend church/synagogue, apart from weddings, funerals, and special
holidays?

Yes. 1   (48)
No . . . . .2 GO TO Q.11

10a. IF YES: How old were you when you stopped attending church/
synagogue? IF NEEDED: Except for weddings, funerals, and special
holidays?

Age when stopped attending:_____ (49–50)

10b. Did you ever start attending church/synagogue again?

Yes. 1   (51)
No . . . . .2 GO TO Q.11

10c. How old were you when you began attending again?

Age began attending again:_____ (52–53)

11. Would you say you are more involved in a church/synagogue now
than you were five years ago? Or would you say less involved, or
about the same?

More involved 1
Less involved 2   (54)
About the same. 3

55 TO 60 BLANK

PART II

Let me ask a few background questions, just to be sure we have a good
cross-section of respondents.

12. Do you have any children?

Yes. 1   (61)
No . . . . 2 GO TO Q.13

12a. IF YES: How many?   Number of children _____   (62–63)

13.   Are you currently . . . READ:

Married. 1
Widowed 2
Divorced 3   (64)
Separated 4
Or have you never been married? . . . 5

14.   In what state or country were you born? RECORD VERBATIM.

Country/state:_____   (65–67)

IF BORN OUTSIDE U.S., GO TO Q.15.

14a. IF BORN IN U.S.: Were both your parents born in this country?
      PROBE IF NECESSARY.

Yes, both 1
One in U.S., one not in U.S. 2   (68)
Neither born in U.S. 4

15.   From what countries or part of the world did your ancestors come?
      RECORD FIRST FOUR MENTIONS.
      IF DON'T KNOW; GO TO Q.17.

_____   (69–71)

_____   (72–74)

_____   (75–77)

_____   (78–80)

15a. IF MORE THAN ONE COUNTRY NAMED IN Q.15: Which one of these coun-
      tries do you feel closest to?

_____   (81–83)

16.   Would you say, in general, that you feel pretty close to other people
      from the same national background, or that you don't feel much closer
      to them than to other people?

Feel closer to them. 1
Don't feel closer to them 2   (84)
FEEL CLOSER TO OTHERS. 3

17. ASK ONLY IF EVER MARRIED, WIDOWED, SEPARATED, OR DIVORCED, Q.13. IF NEVER MARRIED, GO TO Q.18. From what countries or part of the world did your spouse's ancestors come? RECORD FIRST FOUR MENTIONS.

_____ (85–87)

_____ (88–90)

_____ (91–93)

_____ (94–96)

17a. IF MORE THAN ONE COUNTRY NAMED IN Q.17: Which one of the countries does/did your spouse feel closest to?

_____ (97–99)

18. In which state or country were you living when you were 16 years old?

_____ (100–102)

19. And how long have you lived in the area where you live now?

_____ Years (103–104)

20. What was the last grade you completed in school?

_____ Grade (105–106)

21. Last week were you . . . READ:

Working full time 01
Working part time 02   (107–108)
Going to school. . . . . 03 ⎤ GO TO
Keeping house . . . . 04 ⎦ Q.22
Or something else? (SPECIFY)

_____ 05

21a. IF WORKING FULL OR PART TIME, RETIRED, OR UNEMPLOYED: What kind of work do you (did you normally) do? PROBE FOR JOB DESCRIPTION,

RECORD VERBATIM. _____ (109–111)

22. ASK ONLY IF MARRIED OR WIDOWED IN Q.13
What kind of work does/did your husband/wife do? PROBE FOR JOB DESCRIPTION.

RECORD VERBATIM. _____ (112–114)

22a. What race do you consider yourself? RECORD VERBATIM.

White 01   (115–116)
Black .02
Hispanic 03
American Indian 04
Other (SPECIFY)

_____ XX

PART III

Now a few questions of a more personal religious sort:

23.   About how often do you pray? (PROBE IF NECESSARY.)

More than once a day. 1
Daily 2
Several times a week 3
About once a week 4   (117)
Less than once a week 5
Never 6

24.   Within the last year, have you, yourself, read any part of the Bible at home?

Yes. 1
No 2   (118)

25.   At your meals at home does anyone say grace or give thanks to God aloud? (PROBE IF NECESSARY.)

Yes, always or usually 1
Yes, sometimes or on
    special occasions 2   (119)
No 3

IF CHRISTIAN (PART 1.Q.2), CONTINUE.
IF JEWISH, NO RELIGION, OR NON-CHRISTIAN, GO TO PART IV.

26.   Would you say that you have been "born again" or have had a "born again" experience—that is, a turning point in your life when you committed yourself to Christ?

Yes. 1   (120)
No 2   (GSS COD

PART IV.   121–125 BLANK

Now I'd like you to think about people you feel really close to—people you could confide in.

27. Think about relatives outside your immediate family, people like cousins, in-laws, and so forth. Are you very close to many of them, a few of them, or hardly any of them?

Not applicable 1
Many 2   (126)
A few 3
Hardly any. 4
(VOLUNTEERED) NONE 5

28. How about people who live in your neighborhood? Are you close to many of them, a few of them, or hardly any of them?

Not applicable 1
Many 2
A few 3   (127)
Hardly any. 4
(VOLUNTEERED) NONE 5

29. What about people you grew up with and went to school with? Do you still feel close to many of them, a few of them, or hardly any of them?

Not applicable 1
Many 2
A few 3   (128)
Hardly any. 4
(VOLUNTEERED) NONE 5

GO TO Q.31 IF RESPONDENT DOES NOT WORK OUTSIDE THE HOME (RETIRED, HOMEMAKER, STUDENT, ETC., Q.21).

30. How about people you work with? (IF NEEDED: Do you feel very close to) many, a few, or hardly any?

Not applicable 1
Many 2
A few 3   (129)
Hardly any. 4
(VOLUNTEERED) NONE 5

GO TO Q.32 IF RESPONDENT NEVER GOES TO CHURCH/SYNAGOGUE, Q.8.

31. How about the people you know at your church/synagogue? How many of them do you feel very close to—many, a few, or hardly any?

> Not applicable 1
> Many 2
> A few 3   (130)
> Hardly any. 4
> (VOLUNTEERED) NONE 5

32. Outside your church, are you active in any clubs or organizations?

> Yes. 1   (131)
> No . . . . .2 GO TO Q.33

32a. IF YES: Could you tell me which ones? (DON'T RECORD CHURCH OR SYN-AGOGUE ORGANIZATIONS. RECORD VERBATIM. PROBE:) any others?

PROBE FOR CORRECT SPELLING IF UNSURE.

> First mentioned _____   (132–133)
>
> Second mentioned _____   (134–135)
>
> Third mentioned _____   (136–137)

IF MORE THAN 3 MENTIONED: RECORD FIRST 3 ABOVE, AND RECORD TOTAL NUMBER OF MENTIONS (INCLUDING THE THREE ABOVE).

> Total number of organizations mentioned_____   (138–139)

33. Now think of *all* your really close friends—relatives, co-workers, friends from school and church, and so forth. How many of *them* know *each other*—nearly all of them, most of them, or only a few of them?

> Nearly all 1
> Most. 2
> Only a few. 3   (140)
> NONE 4

34. How many of them live right in your local area—nearly all of them, most of them, or only a few of them?

> Nearly all 1
> Most. 2
> Only a few. 3   (141)
> NONE 4

35. How many of them are from the same national or ethnic background as you—nearly all of them, most of them, or only a few of them?

Nearly all 1
Most. 2   (142)
Only a few. 3
NONE 4

36. How many of them attend a church or synagogue on a regular basis?

Nearly all 1
Most. 2   (143)
Only a few. 3
NONE . . . . 4 GO TO Q.37

36a. (IF RESPONDENT GOES TO CHURCH/SYNAGOGUE, Q.8): How many of them attend *your* church/synagogue on a regular basis—nearly all of them, most of them, or only a few of them?

Nearly all 1
Most. 2
Only a few. 3   (144)
NONE 4

37. Some people we talk with in your area think of themselves as . . .

NORTH CAROLINA: Southerners
CALIFORNIA: Westerners
OHIO: Midwesterners
MASSACHUSETTS: New Englanders

READ ONLY ONE.

. . . others don't. How about you? Would you say that you're a REGION NAME or not?

Yes. 1   (145)
No . . . . 2 GO TO PART V

37a. IF YES: Would you say you feel pretty close to [Southerners/Westerners/Midwesterners/New Englanders] in general, or that you don't feel much closer to them than to other people?

Feel closer 1
Do not feel closer 2   (146)
(VOLUNTEERED) FEEL CLOSER TO OTHER PEOPLE 3

PART V.   147–150 BLANK

Here are some more questions about religion:

Please tell me if you agree or disagree with the following statements.

IF UNSURE: All things considered, do you tend to agree or disagree with . . . ?

ROTATE.   AGREE   DISAGREE

38. Most churches and synagogues today
    have lost the real spiritual part
    of religion.   1   2   (151)

39. Most religious congregations are
    warm and accepting to outsiders.   1   2   (152)

40. The rules about morality preached
    by churches and synagogues today
    are just too restrictive.   1   2   (153)

41. An individual should arrive at his
    or her own religious beliefs independent
    of any church or synagogue   1   2   (154)

42. Science and religion will always be in
    conflict.   1   2   (155)

43. The Bible is the actual word of God and is
    to be taken literally, word for word.   1   2   (156)

44. A good Christian or Jew should follow
    his or her conscience, even if it means going
    against what organized religion teaches.   1   2   (157)

45. Being a church member is an important
    way to become established in a community. . . .   1   2   (158)

PART VI.

Here are a few questions about politics:

46. Would you describe your overall political views as . . . READ:

                         Extremely liberal 1
                         Liberal 2
                         Moderate. 3   (159)
                         Conservative 4
                         Or extremely conservative 5   (GSS COD

47. Which presidential candidate do you intend to vote for?

                0   George Bush the Republican

ROTATE.   0   Michael Dukakis the Democrat

> George Bush 1
> Michael Dukakis 2
> SOMEONE ELSE 3   (160)
> Will not vote 4
> Or don't you plan to vote?

48. Do you think labor unions in this country have too much power or too little power?

> Too much. 1
> Too little 2   (161)
> (VOLUNTEERED) ABOUT RIGHT 3

49. Should the federal government spend more money on welfare, or should it spend less?

> More 1
> Less 2   (162)
> (VOLUNTEERED) SAME 3

50. Should it spend more on defense, or should it spend less?

> More 1
> Less 2   (163)
> (VOLUNTEERED) SAME 3

51. Should it spend more or less on protecting the environment?

> More 1
> Less 2   (164)
> (VOLUNTEERED) SAME 3

Here are some more questions about religion:

Do you believe in . . . READ:

	YES	NO	
52. Eternal life	1	2	(165)
53. Reincarnation (that is, we've had previous lives)	1	2	(166)
54. The devil (that is, Satan)	1	2	(167)
55. Astrology (that is, that the stars affect our destiny) . . .	1	2	(168)
56. Ghosts	1	2	(169)

57. Here's a different question. Do you practice any meditation techniques, like those taught by Transcendental Meditation, Zen, the Divine Light Mission, or others?

                              Yes 1   (170)
                              No 2

58. Do most members of your family, or the people you live with, share your views about religion?

                              Yes 1
                              No 2   (171)
                              Not applicable (live alone) 3

59. How about the people you're with every day—that is, people outside your family—do most of them share your views about religion?

                              Yes 1
                              No 2   (172)

60. How important would you say religion generally is in your own life? Is it . . . READ:

                              Very important 1
                              Fairly important 2   (173)
                              Not very important 3

61. We're interested in how people think about churches. Do you think of church/synagogue more as a place to worship in community with friends, or do you think of it more as a place to be alone with God?

                              Place to worship with friends 1
                              Place to be alone with God 2
          (VOLUNTEERED) BOTH EQUALLY, EACH AT   (174)
                              DIFFERENT TIMES, ETC. 3
                    NOT APPLICABLE, CAN'T SAY 4

62. Do you see church as something passed on from generation to generation, or as something that needs to be freely chosen by each person?

                              Something passed on 1
                              Freely chosen 2
          (VOLUNTEERED) COMBINATION, ETC. 3   (175)
                    NOT APPLICABLE, CAN'T SAY 4

63. When you think of church, do you think of something that's always changing, or as something that changes very little?

Always changing. 1
Changes very little. 2   (176)
(VOLUNTEERED) COMBINATION, ETC. 3
NOT APPLICABLE, CAN'T SAY 4

64. Do you believe a person can be a good Christian or Jew if he or she doesn't attend church or synagogue?

Yes. 1
No 2   (177)

65. Can someone be a good Christian or Jew if he or she has doubts whether God exists?

Yes. 1
No 2   (178)

PART VIII.   179–185 BLANK

Do you agree or disagree with the following statements:
IF UNSURE: All things considered, do you tend to agree or disagree with . . . ?

ROTATE   AGREE   DISAGREE

66. Commitment to a meaningful career is one
of the most important things in life   1   2   (186)

67. People who question the old and accepted
ways of doing things usually just end
up causing trouble.   1   2   (187)

68. People have God within them, so churches
aren't really necessary.   1   2   (188)

69. Relationships with family and friends
are more important than what one does
in one's work   1   2   (189)

70. A married woman who doesn't want any more
children should be able to obtain
a legal abortion.   1   2   (200)

71. Do you believe that sexual relations before marriage are *always* morally wrong, *usually* morally wrong, or only *sometimes* morally wrong?

       Always 1
       Usually 2
       Only sometimes 3   (201)
       (VOLUNTEERED) NEVER WRONG. 4

72. How about homosexual relations? Are they *always* morally wrong, *usually* morally wrong, or only *sometimes* morally wrong?

       Always 1
       Usually 2   (202)
       Only sometimes 3
       (VOLUNTEERED) NEVER WRONG. 4

73. How about the death penalty? is it *always* morally wrong, *usually* morally wrong, or only *sometimes* morally wrong?

       Always 1
       Usually 2   (203)
       Only sometimes 3
       (VOLUNTEERED) NEVER WRONG. 4

74. How about cheating on your taxes? Is it *always* morally wrong, *usually* morally wrong, or only *sometimes* morally wrong?

       Always 1
       Usually 2   (204)
       Only sometimes 3
       (VOLUNTEERED) NEVER WRONG. 4

75. How about abortion? Is it *always* morally wrong, *usually* morally wrong, or only *sometimes* morally wrong?

       Always 1
       Usually 2
       Only sometimes 3   (205)
       (VOLUNTEERED) NEVER WRONG. 4

76. How about overthrowing the government? Is it *always* morally wrong, *usually* morally wrong, or only *sometimes* morally wrong?

       Always 1
       Usually 2
       Only sometimes 3   (206)
       (VOLUNTEERED) NEVER WRONG. 4

PART IX.

Just a few more questions.
Please tell me if you agree or disagree with each of these statements:
IF UNSURE: All things considered, do you tend to agree or disagree?

ROTATE   AGREE   DISAGREE

77. Some equality in marriage is a good thing,
    but by and large the husband ought to have
    the main say-so in family matters.   1   2   (207)

78. Despite all the newspapers and TV coverage,
    national and international happenings rarely
    seem as interesting as things that happen
    in your own community.   1   2   (208)

79. I have greater respect for people who are
    well established in their hometowns than
    for people who are widely known, but who
    have no local roots.   1   2   (209)

80. Having a job outside the home is good for a
    married woman because it gives her more of a
    chance to develop as a person   1   2   (210)

81. People owe it to themselves to be the best
    they can in their job or career, even if it
    means they have less time for other people.   1   2   (211)

82. I support the ordination of women, that is, I
    think women should be allowed to be ministers. .   1   2   (212)

83. Finally, one last question: If you could live anywhere you wanted,
    where would you live? PROBE AND READ IF NECESSARY.

                              Same community. 1
                              Same state, different community 2   (213)
                              Different state in U.S.

RECORD VERBATIM: _____). XXX

                              Foreign Country   (214–216)

RECORD VERBATIM: _____). XXX

RECORD LAST 3 DIGITS OF COUNTY CODE FROM CALL SHEET:_____   (217–219)

REPLICATE _____   PAGE NUMBER: _____

TELEPHONE NUMBER: (_____) _____ – _____

_____

END.

Thank you for participating in this important study.

ASK EVERYONE:

We may want to follow up these questions sometimes in the future. If we do, may we contact you again?

Yes. 1
No 2   (220)

IF YES: Please give me your full name.

_____ NAME

CONFIRM PHONE NUMBER.

Thanks again, good evening.

RECORD WHETHER ELIGIBLE RESPONDENT AGREES TO FOLLOW-UP INTERVIEW ON FIRST PAGE OF QUESTIONNAIRE.

FINAL VERSION: 9/27/88

Appendix C

The Research Process

In fall 1987 I approached Robert W. Lynn of the Lilly Endowment about the possibility of funding a study of mainstream American religion with a focus on how different churches in different regions were responding to challenges arising from the 1960s. Data for the whole nation were available, as were case studies of both successful and unsuccessful churches, but common sense suggested that there would be regional differences in the cultural response to the '60s and that these regional differences would also reveal an interesting picture. For example, forces contributing to either growth or decline were probably differentially experienced according to such things as the amount of mobility, the importance of ethnicity, or the degree of countercultural impact found in any region. Surely, I surmised, such forces, combined with the denominational history and current profile of a region, have influenced the current scene. But how? I had speculated about these matters in 1987 in a presidential address to the Society for the Scientific Study of Religion, "Religion and the Persistence of Identity," later published in that society's *Journal* (1988), but more detailed investigation would require some original data.

Not only did Lynn express interest in my proposal, but he also made it possible to submit my proposal in tandem with the proposal of my friend (and now departmental colleague) W. Clark Roof. Roof's interest was specifically on the religious leanings of the so-called baby boomers, those many persons born during the two decades following World War II. The question underlying my project—What is happening to American mainstream religion in various regions?—was clearly linked to the question of what these baby boomers, now grown up, married, and producing children, were doing about religion. We conceived of a three-stage research process, beginning with a telephone survey of 2,600 randomly selected persons between the ages of 25 and 60 in four states. Conducted in fall 1988, this survey concluded with nearly twice the number of persons born between 1945 and 1963 (the baby boomers) as were born during the eighteen years prior. The survey was designed by Roof and me, with the assistance of John Shelton Reed of the University of North Carolina. It was carried out by a commercial firm in Chapel Hill, FGI Inc., over the course of about two months, and the results landed on our two desks just before the end of 1988.

Roof immediately drew a subsample of 536 baby boomers, designed a more detailed questionnaire, and reinterviewed them by telephone. A smaller number (65) of this subsample were then interviewed in person, thus providing rich information about the religious odysseys of these people, a story that Roof is currently writing and will publish in a separate book. Meanwhile, the first batch of telephone interviews were mine to analyze for regional and other differences. *Religion and Personal Autonomy* is the outcome of this analysis.

I was aided by my assistant, Mark Shibley, a graduate student in sociology at UCSB. Involved from the planning stage onward, Mark helped me devise the major measuring devices. These are indexes measuring those main variables that, from the beginning, I had theorized would make for big differences among our respondents. Most of these worked about as I expected—the Morality Index, the Parish Involvement Index, the Local Ties Index, etc. Several measures did not perform as expected, however. For example, believing that ethnic parishes still played a major role, especially in Roman Catholicism, and therefore ethnic identity would be a big factor in parish involvement, we discovered instead that strength of ethnic identity hardly registered in our analysis. It isn't that strong ethnic identity has disappeared among Catholics; rather, whether it has disappeared or not seems to make little difference in Catholic religious beliefs and behavior. Another measure that was surprisingly weak was membership in voluntary associations. First of all, only 36 percent belonged to any voluntary association other than a church, and only one half of these belonged to more than one. The result was little variation among individuals. We had anticipated finding people ranged along a continuum from those persons having largely ascribed, primary group memberships (of which the church, with collective-expressive meaning for such persons, would be one) to those having largely single-purpose, secondary group memberships (of which the church, with individual-expressive meaning for these other persons, would be one.) This scheme was not to be, however, because the number of voluntary association memberships was so meager and yielded so little variation.

A third measurement disappointment was the failure of our "church meaning" items to reveal interpretable distinctions, a failure discussed in chapter 4 above. Since this area of measurement was critical to the originating theory of a new plateau in the disestablishment process, we were fortunate to have included in the interview schedule enough other items that substitute measures could be devised.

As it turned out, then, the major relationships being investigated were found to be pretty much as expected, with some of the secondary hypotheses not supported. The credibility of the whole presentation rests on more than demonstrating significant quantitative relationships, however. The degree to which the various parts of the argument fit together theoretically, for example, is an important criterion. So is the degree to which patterns found today make sense in terms of what is known about yesterday—a kind of cultural transmission perspective. Hence the concern here for the historical record. A third criterion is thus whether the regional differences we found not only uphold the theory as advanced but also represent the sort of differences we would expect from regions with those histories.

We selected four states to study—Massachusetts as a region where ethnicity, we thought, would still be a religious influence; North Carolina, where Conservative Protestantism was and still is a major force; California, where church involvement is modest but religious experimentation is considerable; and Ohio because of its reputation as a "middling" region, representative of the entire United States. The interviewing agency used a random digit dialing procedure to get a sample of 650 adults between the ages of 25 and 60 in each state. The typical refusal rate for telephone surveys of this sort is about one-third, many persons being unwilling to interrupt their meals or other activities for the required time. Most refusals, in other words, are not based on objection to the survey's subject matter but on a general unwillingness to cooperate. North Carolinians, by this reckoning, were most cooperative and people in Massachusetts least cooperative. To get 650 interviews in this latter state required nearly 2,000 phone contacts, as almost two-thirds refused to be interviewed. Several comments can be made about this unusually high refusal rate. First, the interviewers were Southerners primarily, and Massachusetts in October 1988 was the home of the Democratic presidential candidate; many were suspicious of all pollsters, especially those with Southern drawls who wanted to talk about religion and politics. Second, based on later callbacks to persons who had refused to be interviewed, the survey agency determined that most refusals were simply dismissing the importance of the interview. Indeed, when some of these persons were later offered $5 as a symbol of the importance to us of their inclusion in the random sample, they agreed to be interviewed, even though only three of those people actually wanted the $5. Third, it seems unlikely that the higher-than-average refusal rate systematically biased the results. We may not have truly representative subsamples of subpopulations if, for example, Catholics or the divorced or the young or blue-collar workers were less (or more) inclined to be cooperative, but this unrepresentativeness would not disrupt any real relationship between any of these characteristics and people's parish involvement or the meaning they attach to that involvement. Our interest, in other words, is not in *describing the amount* of one or another characteristic but in determining the existence and strength of *relationships between characteristics*.

One major concern, therefore, is to measure with sensitivity those characteristics that are of interest. Where possible we use multiple-item indexes, especially when measuring people's "dispositions"—to be traditional in morality, for example, or to regard parish involvement as a matter of individual choice. For some measures—for instance, age—a single question is adequate, but for others we must ask a number of probing questions, learn how answers fit together, and then combine two or more of those answers into an index. The Parish Involvement Index, described in some detail in chapter 2, is a good illustration of this process.

How does one know if such a measuring index really works? Much has been written about the so-called validity of an index (Does it measure what is claimed for it?) and about its so-called reliability (Is it consistent in what it measures?). For our purposes it is more useful to think of these two features of an index together as the "meaningfulness" of that index. Is it believable? Does its relationship with other measures help make sense of a complex situation? For this reason, we have introduced every index in this book not only by describing how it was constructed but also by showing a number of things related to it, things that common sense suggests *should* be related if the index means what we claim it means.

In place of measures of statistical significance—quantitative devices for assessing the likelihood that results are not "real" but could have occurred by random chance—we usually look for patterns of consistency in the findings. (A measure of statistical significance does appear in Table III–4.) Instead of focusing on one square of the quilt, so to speak, trying to determine from that single square what the quilt means, we look at the whole quilt by examining the way each square relates to every other square. One of the most effective ways of doing this is to make one's argument more convincing by ruling out alternative arguments. Perhaps the clearest use of this strategy is found in chapter 6 (Tables VI–6 and VI–7), where differences between states in rates of pious practices and orthodox beliefs are shown *not* to be artifacts of different proportions of Protestants and Catholics in the several states.

Analysis was carried out from January 1989 through September 1990, and proto-chapters (often beginning as memos) were produced along the way. In retrospect I failed to anticipate fully enough the key role that was to be played in this analysis by the sociocultural revolution of the 1960s and '70s. Of course, the significant changes that get summarized here as "the third disestablishment" were known to have emerged from that volatile period in American life, but the basic thesis of this book—that weakened local ties and adoption of an alternative morality have altered the meaning of involvement in the church—would have been even more convincingly put forward if I had had measures of differential exposure to that period. As it is, I have nothing but logic to link the revolution to the two major effects I assign to it. I am pleased to report that my colleague Roof did ask several questions in the second-wave interviews about such exposure (e.g., participation in demonstrations, smoking marijuana), and he has found such exposure is strongly correlated with such variables as dropout rates and (inversely) with current church involvement rates, thus suggesting what this study would have found had an "exposure" measure been included.

Persons who have little experience with quantitative data analysis in the social sciences will, on occasion, claim that "statistics" can prove anything. Nothing is further from the truth. Data are notorious for being recalcitrant in the hands of the sociologist who is counting on them to tell a particular story. While it is true that, given the same set of data, no two analysts will emerge with exactly the same interpretation, it can nonetheless be safely assumed that—if they are honest—their interpretations will not and cannot be contradictory. Data cannot be forced to lie.

The story being told here can therefore be regarded as on the cautious side because of sampling errors, errors of respondent misunderstanding, coding errors, or errors of oversight. What has been found and reported in this study is so *in spite of* all the obstacles in the way of the "real" interpretation; if it errs, therefore, it errs on the conservative side.

References

Albanese, Catherine L. 1981.
America: Religions and Religion. Belmont, CA.: Wadsworth Publishing Co.

Alberoni, Francesco. 1984.
Movement and Institution. Trans. P. C. Arden Delmoro. New York: Columbia University Press.

Alexander, Katherine. forthcoming.
Catholicism in California.

Allbeck, Willard Dow. 1905.
A Century of Lutherans in Ohio. Yellow Springs, OH: Antioch Press.

Ballard, Harlan H. 1966.
"Western Massachusetts (1789–1861)" in A. B. Hart, ed. *Commonwealth History of Massachusetts*. New York: Russell and Russell.

Beckford, James A. 1989.
Religion and Advanced Industrial Society. London: Unwin Hyman.

Bellah, Robert. 1964.
"Religious Evolution." *American Sociological Review* 29: 358–74.
——— . 1987.
"Competing Visions of the Role of Religion in American Society" in R. Bellah and F. Greenspan, eds., *Uncivil Religion: Interreligious Hostility in America*. New York: Crossroad. 219–32.
——— . 1985.
Habits of the Heart. Berkeley and Los Angeles: University of California Press.

Berger, Peter L. 1967.
The Sacred Canopy. Garden City, NY: Doubleday.

Bernikow, Louise. 1987.
Alone in America. London: Faber and Faber.

Bibby, Reginald. 1987.
Fragmented Gods. Toronto: Irwin Publishing.

Caplow, Theodore, et al. 1983.
All Faithful People. Minneapolis: University of Minnesota Press.

Clecak, P. 1983.
America's Quest for the Ideal Self. New York: Oxford University Press.

Connor, R. D. W. 1929.
    North Carolina: Rebuilding an Ancient Commonwealth (1584–1925).
    Chicago: American Historical Society.
Cox, Harvey. 1965.
    The Secular City. New York: Macmillan.
D'Antonio, W. V., and J. Aldous, eds. 1983.
    Families and Religions: Conflict and Change in Modern Society. Beverly
    Hills: Sage Publications.
D'Antonio, W. V., et al. 1989.
    American Catholic Laity. Kansas City, MO: Sheed and Ward.
Dobbelaere, Karel, and Liliane Voye. 1990.
    "From Pillar to Postmodernity: The Changing Situation of Religion
    in Belgium." *Sociological Analysis* 51, suppl.: S1-S13.
Durkheim, Emile. 1961.
    The Elementary Forms of Religious Life. Trans. J. W. Swain. New York:
    Collier.
Elazar, Daniel J. 1972.
    American Federalism: A View from the States. 2nd ed. New York:
    Crowell.
Ernst, Eldon G. 1986.
    "Religion in California." *Pacific Theological Review* 29 (Winter):
    43–51.
———. 1987.
    Without Help or Hindrance. 2nd ed. Lanham, MD: University Press
    of America.
———. forthcoming.
    Protestantism in California.
Fern, William W. 1917.
    "The Revolt Against the Standing Order" in *The Religious History of
    New England.* Cambridge: Harvard University Press, 75–134.
Ferrier, William W. 1968.
    "The Origin and Growth of the Protestant Church on the Pacific
    Coast" in Charles Sumner Nash, and Wright Buckham Hohn, eds.
    Religious Progress on the Pacific Slope. Freeport, NY: Books for Librar-
    ies Press. 49–81.
Finke, Roger. 1990.
    "Religious Deregulation: Origins and Consequences," *Journal of
    Church and State* 32 (Summer): 609–26.
Finke, Roger, and Rodney Stark. 1992.
    The Churching of America, 1776–1990. New Brunswick, NJ: Rutgers
    University Press.

Fitzgerald, Frances. 1986.
   Cities on a Hill. New York: Simon and Schuster.
Frankiel, Sandra Sizer. 1988.
   California's Spiritual Frontiers: Religious Alternatives in Anglo-Protestantism, 1850–1910. Berkeley and Los Angeles: University of California Press.
Gratzer, Walter, ed. 1989.
   The Longman Literary Companion to Science. Essex, England: Longman Group.
Greeley, Andrew M. 1989.
   Religious Change in America. Cambridge, MA: Harvard University Press.
———. 1990.
   The Catholic Myth. New York: Scribner's.
Greeley, Andrew M., et al. 1976.
   Catholic Schools in a Declining Church. Kansas City, MO: Sheed and Ward.
Hale, Edward Everett. 1966.
   "Religious and Social Reforms (1820–1861)" in A. B. Hart, ed. *Commonwealth History of Massachusetts.* New York: Russell and Russell, 252–78.
Hammond, Phillip E. 1986.
   "The Extravasation of the Sacred and the Crisis in Liberal Protestantism" in Robert Michaelsen and W. Clark Roof, eds. *Liberal Protestantism: Realities and Prospects.* New York: Pilgrim Press.
———. 1988.
   "Religion and the Persistence of Identity." *Journal for the Scientific Study of Religion* 27 (Mar.): 1–11.
Handy, Robert T. 1984.
   A Christian America. 2nd ed. New York: Oxford University Press.
Harrington, Michael. 1983.
   The Politics at God's Funeral. New York: Penguin.
Hatch, Nathan O. 1980.
   "The Christian Movement and the Demand for a Theology of the People." *The Journal of American History* 67 (Dec.): 545–67.
Hecht, Richard, et al. forthcoming.
   Diaspora in Paradise.
Herberg, Will. 1955.
   Protestant, Catholic, Jew. Garden City, NY: Doubleday.
Hill, Samuel S. 1966.
   Southern Churches in Crisis. New York: Holt, Rinehart.

Hill, Samuel S., ed. 1983.
  Religion in the Southern States. Macon, GA: Mercer University Press.
  ——— . 1988.
  Varieties of Southern Religious Experience. Baton Rouge: Louisiana
  State University Press.
Hoge, Dean, and David Roozen, eds. 1979.
  Understanding Church Growth and Decline: 1950–1978. New York: Pil-
  grim Press.
Hogue, Harland E. 1976.
  "The Protestant Churches" in Francis J. Weber, ed., *The Religious
  Heritage of Southern California: A Bicentennial Survey*. Los Angeles:
  Interreligious Council of Southern California, 75–84.
Hunt, Morton. 1974.
  Sexual Behavior in the 1970s. Chicago: Playboy Press.
Huthmacher, J. Joseph. 1959.
  Massachusetts: People and Politics 1919–1933. Cambridge, MA:
  Belknap Press.
Kasarda, John D., and Morris Janowitz. 1974.
  "Community Attachment in Mass Society." *American Sociological
  Review* 39: 328–39.
Kennedy, Eugene. 1988.
  Tomorrow's Catholics, Yesterday's Church. New York: Harper and Row.
Lefler, Hugh T., et al. 1973.
  The History of a Southern State: North Carolina. Chapel Hill: Univer-
  sity of North Carolina Press.
Lord, Robert Howard. 1966.
  "The Catholic Church in Massachusetts" in A. B. Hart, ed., *Com-
  monwealth History of Massachusetts*. New York: Russell and Russell,
  504–37.
Luckmann, Thomas. 1967.
  The Invisible Religion. New York: Macmillan.
Lynd, Robert S., and Helen M. Lynd. 1929.
  Middletown. New York: Harcourt, Brace.
McGuire, Meredith. 1987.
  Religion: The Social Context. Belmont, CA: Wadsworth.
  ——— . 1988.
  Ritual Healing in Suburban America. New Brunswick, NJ: Rutgers
  University Press.
McLoughlin, William G. 1978.
  Revivals, Awakenings, and Reform. Chicago: University of Chicago
  Press.

McNamara, Patrick. 1991.
   Conscience First, Tradition Second: A Study of Young American Catholics. Albany: State University of New York Press.
McTighe, Michael J. 1988.
   "Babel and Babylon on the Cuyahoga: Religious Diversity in Cleveland" in Thomas F. Campbell and Edward M. Miggins, eds., *The Birth of Modern Cleveland, 1865–1930.* Cleveland: Western Reserve Historical Society, 231–69.
Mathews, Donald G. 1969.
   "The Second Great Awakening as an Organizing Process, 1780–1830." *American Quarterly* 21: 23–43.
Mead, Sidney E. 1977.
   The Old Religion in the Brave New World. Berkeley and Los Angeles: University of California Press.
Miyakawa, T. Scott. 1964.
   Protestants and Pioneers: Individualism and Conformity on the American Frontier. Chicago: University of Chicago Press.
Mol, Hans, ed. 1978.
   Identity and Religion. Beverly Hills: Sage Publications.
Morris, C. R. 1984.
   A Time of Passion. Harmondsworth: Penguin.
Nelsen, Hart M., Raytha L. Yokley, and Anne K. Nelsen, eds. 1971.
   The Black Church in America. New York: Basic Books.
Neuhaus, Richard John. 1984.
   The Naked Public Square. Grand Rapids: Eerdmans.
Niebuhr, H. Richard. 1929.
   The Social Sources of Denominationalism. New York: Henry Holt.
Nisbet, Robert. 1953.
   Community and Power. New York: Oxford University Press.
Odum, Howard W., and H. E. Moore. 1938.
   American Regionalism. New York: Holt, Rinehart.
Packard, Vance. 1972.
   A Nation of Strangers. New York: McKay.
Parsons, Talcott. 1963.
   "Christianity and Modern Industrial Society" in E. A. Tiryakian, ed., *Sociological Theory, Values and Sociocultural Change.* Glencoe, IL: Free Press.
Perin, Constance. 1988.
   Belonging in America. Madison: University of Wisconsin Press.
Pershing, Benjamin H. 1941.
   "Religion in the Twentieth Century" in Harlow Lindley, ed., *The*

History of the State of Ohio: Ohio in the Twentieth Century 1900–1938. Columbus: Ohio State Historical Society, 354–85.

Platner, John Winthrop. 1917.
"The Congregationalists" in J. W. Platner and others, *The Religious History of New England*. Cambridge: Harvard University Press, 1–74.

Powell, William S. 1989.
North Carolina Through Four Centuries. Chapel Hill: University of North Carolina Press.

Quinn, Bernard, et al. 1982.
Churches and Church Membership in the United States, 1980. Atlanta: Glenmary Research Center.

Reichley, A. James. 1985.
Religion in American Public Life. Washington: The Brookings Institute.

Roof, W. Clark. 1978.
Community and Commitment. New York: Elsevier.
——— . 1979.
"Concepts and Indicators of Religious Commitment: A Critical Review" in Robert Wuthnow, ed., *The Religious Dimension*. New York: Academic Press.
——— . 1988a.
"On Bridging the Gap Between Social Scientific Methodology and Religious Studies." *Soundings* 71 (Summer/Fall): 295–314.
——— . 1988b.
"Religious Change in the American South: The Case of the Un-churched" in Samuel S. Hill, ed., *Varieties of Southern Religious Experience*. Baton Rouge: Louisiana State University Press. 192–210.

Roof, W. Clark, and W. McKinney. 1987.
American Mainline Religion. New Brunswick, NJ: Rutgers University Press.

Roseboom, Eugene, et al. 1967.
A History of Ohio. Columbus: Ohio Historical Society.

Royce, Josiah. 1958.
California from the Conquest in 1846 to the Second Vigilance Committee in San Francisco. New York: Houghton, Mifflin.

Ruthven, Malise. 1989.
The Divine Supermarket. London: Chatto and Windus.

Seidler, John, and Katherine Meyer. 1989.
Conflict and Change in the Catholic Church. New Brunswick, NJ: Rutgers University Press.

Singleton, Gregory H. 1977.

Religion in the City of Angels: American Protestant Culture and Urbanization, Los Angeles 1850–1930. Ann Arbor: UNI Research Press.

Slattery, Charles Lewis. 1966.

"Religious Forces (1889–1929)" in A. B. Hart, ed., *Commonwealth History of Massachusetts.* New York: Russell and Russell. 455–76.

Stark, Rodney, and C. Y. Glock. 1968.

American Piety. Berkeley and Los Angeles: University of California Press.

Stark, Rodney, and Roger Finke. 1988.

"American Religion in 1776: A Statistical Portrait." *Sociological Analysis* 49, 1: 39–51.

Starr, Kevin. 1973.

Americans and the California Dream. New York: Oxford University Press.

———. 1985.

Inventing the Dream. New York: Oxford University Press.

Troeltsch, Ernst. [1911] 1960.

The Social Teaching of the Christian Churches. Trans. Olive Wyon. New York: Harper.

Wallace, Ruth. 1991.

They Call Her Pastor. Albany: State University of New York Press.

Warner, R. Stephen. 1988.

New Wine in Old Wineskins. Berkeley and Los Angeles. University of California Press.

Waters, Mary C. 1990.

Ethnic Options. Berkeley and Los Angeles: University of California Press.

Welch, Kevin. 1983.

"Community Development and Metropolitan Religious Commitment: A Test of Two Competing Models." *Journal for the Scientific Study of Religion* 22: 167–81.

Welch, Michael R., and J. Baltzell. 1984.

"Geographic Mobility, Social Integration, and Church Attendance." *Journal for the Scientific Study of Religion* 23: 75–90.

Wills, Garry. 1990.

"Mario Cuomo's Trouble with Abortion." *New York Review of Books* June 28: 9ff.

Wilson, Bryan. 1968.

"Religious Organization" in David L. Sills, ed., *International Encyclopedia of the Social Sciences.* New York: Crowell Collier and Macmillan. 13: 428–37.

———. 1982.

Religion in Sociological Perspective. Oxford: Oxford University Press.

Wireman, P. 1984.

Urban Neighborhoods, Networks, and Families. Lexington, MA: Lexington Books.

Woodard, John R. 1983.

"North Carolina" in Samuel S. Hill, ed. *Religion in the Southern States.* Macon, GA: Mercer University Press. 215–38.

Wuthnow, Robert. 1976.

The Consciousness Reformation. Berkeley and Los Angeles: University of California Press.

———. 1978.

Experimentation in American Religion. Berkeley and Los Angeles: University of California Press.

———. 1987.

Meaning and Moral Order. Berkeley and Los Angeles: University of California Press.

———. 1988.

The Restructuring of American Religion. Princeton, NJ: Princeton University Press.

Wuthnow, Robert, and Kevin Christiano. 1979.

"The Effects of Residential Migration on Church Attendance in the United States" in Robert Wuthnow, ed., *The Religious Dimensions.* New York: Academic Press. 257–76.

Yankelovich, Daniel. 1974.

The New Morality. New York: McGraw Hill.

———. 1981.

New Rules. New York: Random House.

Index